The Pearl
and
the Dragon

The Pearl and the Dragon

*The Story of
Alma and Gerhard Jacobson*

S. Winifred Jacobson

Christian Publications, Inc.
Camp Hill, Pennsylvania

Dedicated

to the memory of those China missionaries who, before the communist takeover in 1949, helped form the precious Pearl—the Church in China—which has resulted in the dramatic growth of the Pearl today.

And to their children, grandchildren and great-grandchildren who are following in their train, as well as those who may be inspired to do so by reading this account.

Christian Publications, Inc.
3825 Hartzdale Drive, Camp Hill, PA 17011

Faithful, biblical publishing since 1883

ISBN: 0-87509-700-6

© 1997 by Christian Publications, Inc.

All rights reserved
Printed in the United States of America

97 98 99 00 01   5 4 3 2 1

Unless otherwise indicated,
Scripture taken from the HOLY BIBLE:
NEW INTERNATIONAL VERSION ®.
Copyright © 1973, 1978, 1984 by the
International Bible Society. Used by
permission of Zondervan Bible Publishers.

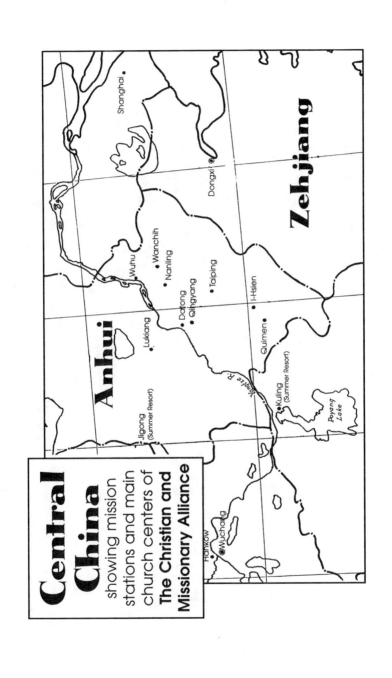

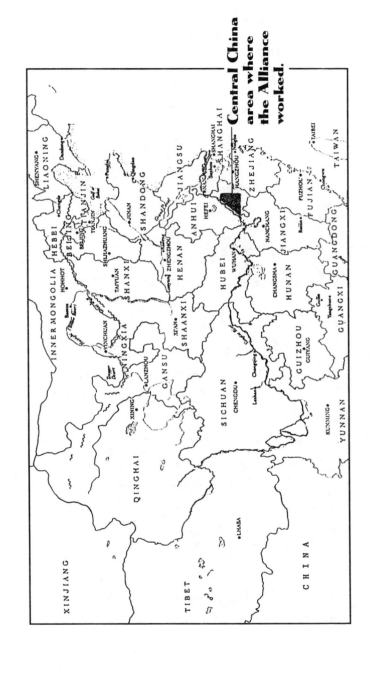

Contents

Acknowledgments ix
Introduction 1
1 The Pearl: A Voice Calling   3
2 Golden Pearls: The Amstutz Heritage   9
3 Selected Pearls: The Jacobson Heritage   17
4 Matching Pearls: Two People, One Prayer   26
5 Matched Pearls: The Decision   33
6 Prepared Pearls: China at Last!   39
7 The Dragon's Claws: A Spiritual Battle   48
8 The Dragon's Power: A Tragic Summer, a New Ministry   56
9 The Dragon's Lair: Datong   71
10 The Dragon's Fury: Taiping   79
11 The Dragon's Fury: The Ultimatum   89
12 The Dragon Is Defeated: "Fear Not"   96
13 The Dragon Is Defeated: A New Attitude, a New Church   108
14 Pearls in the Dragon's Lair: Datong   119
15 The Dragon's Work: Qingyang   128
16 The Dragon's Fangs: Qimen   137
17 The Dragon Attacked: Shanghai   146

18	*Confronted by the Dragon: On the Air*	152
19	*The Dragon Fights: The Rising Sun and the Swastika*	162
20	*The Dragon's Defeat: The Great Escape*	175
21	*The Dragon's Defeat: Together at Last*	182

Epilogue 193
Epilogue 2 196
Epilogue 3 198

Acknowledgments

The *Pearl and the Dragon* is the story of my parents, Gerhard and Alma Jacobson—two people who made themselves expendable for the sake of the gospel in China. Woven together with theirs are also the stories of heroic co-workers of The Christian and Missionary Alliance and some from other missions. Their sacrifice and challenge to North American Christians and prayer warriors aroused in many a love for missions.

My father was a man with a passion for soul-winning who labored intensely for his Master. My mother, who worked along with him, was known as a woman of great faith and prayer.

Next to the gift of salvation itself, and yet closely related to it, is the high privilege of having godly parents and grandparents. In our family this heritage led twelve of their descendants to follow the Lord in full-time missionary service.

Many have contributed to the writing of this book. I am grateful to the staff of Christian Publications for their help and encouragement as well as their willingness to print the story.

Here at the Bradenton Missionary Village, I

wish to thank Hardy Hayes of HCJB, our computer expert who came to the rescue many times to solve computer problems: also Mary Dayton, Child Evangelism Fellowship missionary from the Philippines, who did much of the typing on her computer until she taught me how.

Vonnie Morscheck of The Christian and Missionary Alliance in Indonesia helped with typing and proofreading and allowed me the use of her computer.

Other proofreaders were Margaret Sells, Presbyterian missionary and English teacher from China and Taiwan, and Dr. Viola Waterhouse with Wycliffe Bible Translators from Mexico.

Gladys Peterson, who works with D.C. Cook Ministries, offered many helpful suggestions.

My sisters, Doris, Bette and Evey supplied important data on events and people. Doris also provided me with free time by taking over many household tasks.

Above all I want to thank the Lord. He has shown me in a special way that He is Wisdom. With Him I was able to do much more than my natural abilities would have allowed.

For all who prayed for me, I am most grateful. It is my desire that Christ alone be glorified.

S. Winifred Jacobson
Bradenton, Florida
January, 1995

Introduction

In a small out-of-the-way restaurant in Kowloon, Hong Kong, a fascinating picture catches the eye. Intricately embroidered on silk is a gold and vermillion dragon with its claws reaching out to a pale pink pearl. The dragon's mouth flashes fire, its green orbs gleam greedily. Will the dragon devour the pearl?

The symbols in that picture? China, Land of the Dragon, grasping for Hong Kong, the Pearl of the Orient.

In this book, Satan is the Dragon, and the Pearl is the Church of Jesus Christ in China. Try as he might, the Dragon has failed to destroy the Pearl. Her Keeper is strong, for all the powers of heaven are on His side, just as all the powers of hell are on the side of the Dragon.

It was the desire of my parents, Gerhard and Alma Jacobson, to have a part in discovering pearls in China—precious blood-bought believers who would be a part of the great Pearl—the Church universal.

This is their story.

1

The Pearl: A Voice Calling

The little sideroom smoldered with a deep oppressive kind of darkness, the form of a young man, his face in his hands, barely visible.

The figure shook and swayed, recalling those first terrifying days when many weeks earlier he and Pastor Hu (HOO) had entered Taiping (TIE ping). The whole city had risen up against their presence. Mobs surrounded the house.

"*Sha, sha! Yang guei dze!* Kill, kill the foreign devil," they screamed. Miraculously, Gerhard and Pastor Hu were still there. An official of Taiping, a walled county seat in South Anhui (AHN whay), had declared that they would never allow foreigners to live or buy land there because of the devastation resulting from the Taiping Rebellion.

Without the intervention of a small contingent of guards from the magistrate's headquarters who thwarted the crowd's murderous intent, the mob scene might have ended otherwise. But now the guards—and their protection—were removed.

Gerhard recalled how bravely he and Pastor Hu had set out from Datong (Dah TUNG). He could still see their two families waving and smiling tearfully as the men set out down the road. Now his heart became numb with an agonizing dread—he was jeopardizing his family's future. If the murderous mob returned and had its way, he would leave them fatherless.

The curtains of the sedan chair pushed back as Mrs. Li (LEE), the Bible woman, helped a small young woman and little girl to the street. The chair bearers shouted, driving the crowds away with spicy curses that left embarrassed looks on the sea of dark faces.

"I told you not to come to Taiping," Gerhard shouted above the din. "It's very dangerous here, Alma. Why did you come?"

"The Lord told me to come," his petite wife answered self-assuredly as she picked up a box and headed toward the house.

Pastor Hu dickered with the carriers. Mrs. Li shouted to the men as she directed traffic toward the large reception room where the bags were to be placed. The street seemed enveloped in utter confusion.

Inside, Gerhard bent over the boxes and turned to Alma.

"It's good to see you, darling," he said somewhat more gently, "but it makes the situation worse than ever with you two here."

Out of the corner of his eye he could see the stout Bible woman hobbling on her bound feet, heading for the kitchen where she would, no doubt, command the crew to make tea for the weary travelers.

Suddenly it seemed that all the weariness Gerhard had accumulated over the last three months drained from his body. It was as if his prison-house existence was forever gone. He rushed to the cupboard where his meager household utensils were stored and began to set a square wooden table.

Looking once more at his wife, he paused.

"Well, you always do what you want, Alma," he said with a slight smile. "Anyway, I'm thanking the Lord you arrived today since you did decide to come."

"Why is that, Gay?" Alma asked, using the abbreviation she reserved for intimate discussions with her husband. Then without waiting for a reply, she continued. "This is a nice big room for services, but so dark and stuffy. Can't we open the doors a bit?"

"And have everyone cramming in to stare at us?"

"Oh, yes, of course. We all had to have our skin and hair felt every time people got near enough to touch us as we came into the city. They thought Doris's brown hair was golden."

Alma glanced at the diminutive five-year-old running from corner to corner, delightedly squealing something in Chinese at each new discovery. Her yellow, pongee-silk dress fluttered like butterfly wings in the dark shadows.

"So why did you feel my coming to Taiping today was so providential?" Alma asked again, this time waiting for a reply.

"Actually, my faith was at its lowest point since coming here," Gerhard responded, a painful shadow crossing his face. "I was just sitting on the cot in the next room thinking about how to get out, and . . ."

"You'd never leave after this long a time," Alma interjected. "You're not a stubborn Swede for nothing." Her girlish laugh brought stares from the Chinese nearby.

What a pleasing sight these two missionaries made—Alma with her dark brown hair coiled neatly at the nape of her neck, her softly rounded, heart-shaped face and large expressive blue eyes lending a look of vibrant innocence. She was fanning vigorously, hoping to dry out her silk blouse and black Chinese pants. The pointed cloth shoes hung off her feet. It was cooler that way.

Gerhard was also laughing. To the Chinese he seemed tall and well-built, his face more classic, with a fine straight nose, a sensitive mouth and strong chin. In some ways Gerhard ma were look-alikes, at least to Chinese eyes. Both faces were radiant with the happiness they felt after months of separation.

"Let's have a look at the bedroom and start arranging my things," suggested Alma as she lifted herself out of the hard bamboo chair and followed Gerhard into another dark but spacious room.

There were a few shelves and a large black Chinese cupboard along the wall. Black chairs stood here and there around the room. The bed was just boards set on two trestles. Piled on top was a nicely stuffed straw mattress, along with an assortment of pillows and quilts—*all bought on the street*, Alma decided. Above the bed was a fairly large dark hole.

"Things look very comfortable here. But what is that hole?" Alma asked, pointing to the ceiling. "Does it lead to the attic?"

"Yes. That's where the pet snake stays in the daytime." Gerhard grinned.

"How about at night?"

"He has come and shared my bed with me. Not exactly my idea of a good bedfellow though." Now Gerhard was laughing out loud.

Alma sat down on the bed but she didn't laugh. *And I'm supposed to sleep here?* she thought to herself.

Her mind wandered back to the early years when she and Gerhard had met in Chicago. Now, here they were in the Land of the Dragon. Suddenly Alma looked up at the window. A brilliant sunset was bidding its farewell from behind a crinkled hill.

Oh, there was a fascination about it all. It was as if a voice was calling, "Come see what's behind these far off hills. There's something here for you, something you are looking for."

But what was that something? Could it be the Pearl?

2

Golden Pearls: The Amstutz Heritage

Wedding preparations were well underway, the German-Swiss colony of Mennonites in Pandora, Ohio, astir with excitement. On this day, May 31, 1887, dainty Sarah Lugibihl would be married to Jonathan Amstutz, each the eldest of their respective families.

Children and adults scurried everywhere. Sarah's sisters Mary and Lena ran through the fields gathering mock orange branches with which to decorate the living room of the Abraham Lugibihl farmhouse.

"Pick as many as you can," Mary instructed her sister. "They'll look beautiful with our tulips and lilacs." But the bushes resisted the two black-bonneted girls.

"Here, give me those scissors," said Mary impatiently. "I can cut them faster."

Flopping on the grass, Lena whipped off her bonnet.

"We've got more than we need already," she complained. "Let's go home." Mary's "ya" was enough. They trudged back home, their arms laden with the fragrant blossoms.

On the expansive lawn, under oaks and maples, long tables were already laden with food for the festive occasion. Borrowed silverware and white linen cloths set off fancy china brought from the old country. Luscious odors of frying chicken, beef stew, boiled lamb and even wild venison filled the air. Fancy vegetables, pickles and pastries added the finishing touches.

By mid-morning buggies and wagons began to arrive. Some carried benches for the wedding service. Everyone was dressed in their finest, especially the children whose bows, lace and bonnets had been freshly starched for the occasion. Last to arrive were the pastor and deacons.

Sarah the bride, in silk brocade, stood small and petite beside Jonathan, her handsome groom. A large taffeta bow was at her throat, a delicate bouquet of white roses at her waist. A single white rose graced the groom's lapel.

The service was a long one, so long that the couple sat down as the pastor gave his exhortation. Several deacons also addressed the couple. Finally, after a lengthy wedding hymn, Sarah and Jonathan recited their vows and the feast began.

At first the couple lived in Bluffton where Jonathan and his brother Jonas were part owners of a dry goods store. But Jonathan was more interested in farming. The land in those parts had once been called the Black Swamp. But it had been drained by "enough tiles to circle the globe three times" and most of the forest in the area had been leveled. Jonathan bought land and built a small but sturdy white frame house.

"Sarah, dear," her mother remarked one day, "Jonathan doesn't look well, but being a farmer's wife suits you perfectly. Perhaps," her mother continued, "it might be well for Jonathan to see the doctor. He has so many stomach upsets and fevers."

Sarah sat down awkwardly on a kitchen chair. She looked tired. Her bulky shape foretold another birth in the family.

"Mother," Sarah responded, "Jonathan works so hard in all kinds of weather. He would like to get this farm paid for as soon as possible." Her forehead wrinkled in an anxious frown.

"Just tell him that neither Father nor I want him to work so hard that he ruins his health. You must talk to him. His brother Jonas coughs all the time too. There is tuberculosis in that family, you know."

Mother Lugibihl's thoughts wandered back to the old days when the Amstutz and Lugibihl children were happy playmates. Now one by one the Amstutz boys were courting and marrying her daughters. Sarah had been courted while Jonathan was studying at Ada College. Although she had attended only a few years of elementary school, they seemed well suited.

"I must hurry home," Mother Lugibihl said finally. "I promised the boys a sugar pie for supper." She gathered her cloak and started off across the lane.

With the coming of spring, Sarah noticed that Jonathan seemed to be growing weaker every day. Medicines didn't help. More and more of the farm work fell to her and her brothers while Jonathan spent days and sometimes weeks in bed. When she was not working on the farm, Sarah sat at her husband's side. Waldo, now five, was his mother's right hand, while four-year-old Alma did her best to care for the younger ones—Edna, three years old, and baby Rhoda, six months.

One spring day Waldo and Alma went to gather pussywillows by Riley Creek. Brimming with excitement, they ran back to the house and to their father's bedside.

"Look what we brought for you, Papa," Alma beamed. Jonathan smiled back weakly.

"Will you please sing a song for us?" Alma begged as she dropped the pussywillows onto a nearby chair.

Their daddy began to sing. It was a song about heaven. The children watched and listened as the voice grew faint and finally subsided. Then their father's eyes closed.

"Mother, come quickly," Waldo shouted. By the time Sarah arrived, her husband was no longer breathing.

He's gone. The thought flashed through her mind unbidden. And then reality gripped her heart like a vise: *He really is gone.* Taking Waldo and Alma into her arms, she held them up to kiss the silent form.

"Waldo, please call your Grandfather Lugibihl," she whispered. Alma slipped her hand into her brother's and the two darted down the lane.

Just seven short years, thought Sarah, *and the light has gone out of my life.*

A few days later, although the sun was shining and the song of the first robins filled the air, there was no sun or song for the young widow Sarah Amstutz. Inside, her heart was bleeding, her mind whirling. *What shall I do with my family?* she asked herself. *I have no training.* Staying with her father on the farm provided the answer.

Before Sarah knew it, it was time for the children to enter high school, so she decided to buy a home in Pandora. Changes were taking place among Mennonite families as they came in contact with those of other faiths.

One group, called the Defenseless Mennonites, was led by an itinerant evangelist from Canada named Joseph Ramseyer who came to Pandora to hold special meetings. With him were his sister and brother who provided music for the services. Revival broke out wherever they went.

"We held a few weeks of meetings in the Defenseless Mennonite church between Pandora and Bluffton," Joseph Ramseyer later recounted. "The Holy Spirit moved mightily among us and many came out definitely for the Lord." The widow Sarah Amstutz and her friend Judith Lehman were among them.

A number of years passed and once again a tent was set up outside the Defenseless Mennonite Church. On the evening before the revival started, crying broke out at a service in the church. The whole place was turned into an altar as the meeting lasted far into the night.

Doctrines such as divine healing, the second coming of Christ and baptism by immersion were explained from the Scriptures. Sarah was fascinated.

After much prayer and heart-searching, she decided to join this little group of believers. It later merged with the German branch of The Christian and Missionary Alliance to form the Missionary Church Association.

The year 1900 was a red-letter year. That year, Waldo, who along with Edna and Alma, had also resisted attending his mother's church, began to feel that it was not right for their family to be divided.

"I think we should go with Mother to her church," he advised his sisters one Sunday. They agreed. Sarah was thrilled.

First Alma, Edna and Rhoda found the Lord at the Missionary Church. Then, several nights later when the call was given, Waldo shot out of his seat and found a place among many others at the altar. What rejoicing there was in heaven and around the Amstutz kitchen table that night. Each one of Sarah's children was now safely in the fold.

Meanwhile, Alma enrolled at Wooster College to take a short teacher's course and began her first years of teaching at one of the little red schoolhouses not far from home.

At the Missionary Church events happened so fast that the town was shaken. A Bible school, known as Bethany Bible Institute, with faculty who had been trained at the Nyack Missionary Training Institute, opened with twenty-five boarding students.

Missionary conferences added to the excitement. At one of the most memorable, Nellie Bowen, a newly appointed missionary to China, spoke. People were deeply moved by her stirring testimony and call for prayer partners. Alma placed Nellie's picture in her Bible and prayed for her faithfully.

By now, Sarah's dear friend, Judith Lehman,

was a mission worker to the Jews in Chicago. She invited Sarah to be the hostess for the Mission's new building. So, within days, Mother Sarah and her two daughters Alma and Edna were ready to leave for Chicago.

3

Selected Pearls: The Jacobson Heritage

A saucy little breeze was flirting with the voluminous skirts and kerchiefs of two young ladies as they leaned over the railing of the Cunard steamship gliding into Boston harbor.

Passengers crowded the decks. Cries of surprise were heard everywhere. Tears of joy streamed down happy faces swarthy from the vineyards of Italy, rosy-cheeked from the misty crags of Scotland or snowy-white and golden-haired from the fjords of Scandinavia.

America was suffering from an acute manpower shortage following the civil war. Famine that had raged in Europe for decades made America the Land of Promise. Land-hungry peasants dreamed of someday owning their own farms and being as rich as barons.

"Do you think Anders will be here to meet us?" Anna Louise Swanson asked her sister Minnie.

"Now there you go worrying," her older sister chided. "Just look for a tall man in a red-checkered shirt."

The masses of faces on land came into focus as the ship neared the dock. Suddenly a very tall blonde man in a checkered shirt whipped off his cap and shouted something in Swedish.

"Look, Anna, that man waving his cap! Isn't he shouting at us?" Minnie cried excitedly.

"Yes, Minnie, it's Anders. Anders! Anders!" Anna Louise called at the top of her lungs as she pulled off her kerchief and waved vigorously to the man on the shore.

It took no time to reach the gangplank. There was Anders Gustafson grinning at the bottom of the steps, ready to carry their baggage and help them through customs and quarantine. He would be their guide all the way to Chicago.

That night a group of girls, also from the steamship, gathered around the bunks of Anna Louise and Minnie Swanson.

"Anna and Minnie, you are so fortunate," they complained. "We wish we had a boyfriend and a job waiting for us. We are supposed to be maids, but how will we get along without English?"

"John Jacobson, my fiancé, told me that Pastor Fredrickson, the Lutheran minister from

Rinna, will be there to help us get started in our new lives," Anna told the anxious group surrounding her. "Why don't we read a little from our Bibles and pray together before we go to sleep?"

A fine rain was falling the next day as the train pulled into Chicago. The city looked dismal and gray. Mile after mile of streets and houses, factories and stores flashed past the train's windows. And then, there it was—Union Station under its glass canopy.

It wasn't hard to see John Jacobson. He was taller than most in the crowd.

"Oh, at last you have come!" he exclaimed in Swedish as he grasped both hands of his beloved Anna Louise. "We have arranged for you to stay at our rooming house tonight. Tomorrow, after you have rested, you can see some of the sights of the city and my new tailor shop on Michigan Avenue. How would you like that?" John's sunny smile and jocund manner lifted the spirits of the weary travelers as he helped load baggage into his carriage.

By the end of the nineteenth century and into the early twentieth, great changes were taking place in the life of the ordinary American citizen. Factories in Chicago were filled with farm girls from Ohio and lumberjacks from Minnesota. And, across the nation, Edison's 24 million light bulbs flashed their brilliance at the mere flip of a switch. John Jacobson's tailor shop on Michigan Avenue, benefiting from the new technology, now buzzed and hummed with the sounds of new and cheaper sewing machines.

Minnie and Anna Louise Swanson soon adjusted to life in the Lakeview District of Chicago. After all, on Belmont Avenue hardly a word of English could be heard on Saturday nights. The fish and Swedish pastry shops and cozy coffee houses were just like home.

"Did you know that Pastor Fredrickson plans to perform a wedding for several couples in May?" John asked his fiancée one day as she sat stitching maroon ribbons on the gown of a wealthy customer.

"Yes," Anna blushed as she bit off a thread, "but I thought you wanted to wait until the house on Clifton Avenue was finished."

"Oh, you haven't seen it for a while," John beamed. "Let's take a ride out there after work. You will see how far along it is."

After the shop was cleaned and closed, John helped Anna Louise into the carriage. With a sharp slap of the reins the horse galloped over the cobblestone streets to where a turn into a small side street brought them to a deep vacant lot. At the back was a house under construction.

To Anna Louise's wondering eyes it looked like a mansion. Their parents on both sides had lived in little cottages as tenant farmers in Sweden.

"Oh, and it has three floors. But why did you build the house so far back on the lot, John?"

There was a twinkle in John's blue eyes as he replied.

"Maybe, if the Lord will bless us," he responded, "we can have an apartment building at the front." Anna Louise's eyes grew even wider.

May 1881 came quickly, and what a gala occasion it was at the Swedish Lutheran Church! John beamed with pride as he gazed on the snowy-white skin and periwinkle blue eyes of his bride. Her golden, corn-silk braids circled the ringlets around her face. To him she was truly the fairest, dressed in a sweeping silk gown.

"I pronounce you man and wife," intoned Pastor Fredrickson. With these final words Anna Louise looked up at John Jacobson. She knew that in the old country he had changed his name from Mork to Jacobson. Mork meant "dark" and he had been teased by his friends. There was nothing dark about her John. And then there were his broad shoulders, now thrown back as the church's light reflected in his wavy blonde hair. *He looks as bright as a valiant Viking returning to his land in victory,* Anna thought admiringly.

"We will have a home where God's Word and His Church will be first in our lives just as they were in our homes in Sweden, won't we, Anna?" John asked, looking deep into his wife's glowing eyes.

"Oh, yes," Anna Louise replied, "and I will stand behind you as head of this family."

The couple joined a newly formed congregation just a few blocks from their Clifton Avenue home. Here Anna Louise and John's children Albert and David were baptized in childhood.

When a third child was born into the Jacobson family, Anna said, "I think we should name him George, don't you? It sounds more American."

"Oh, I thought you liked the name Gerhard," John responded. "We're Swedes, remember? And his second name should be Antonius like his uncle's." So it was that the clerk at the Cook County registry wrote, "February 15th, 1889, Gerhard Antonius Jacobson, third son of John Albert and Anna Louise Jacobson." His mother and others, however, called him George.

Three more children would eventually be added to the Jacobson family and, true to the young couple's dream, a three-and-a-half-story brick and frame apartment building would eventually stand in front of the neat white cottage at the back of the lot.

Chicago, a great hub for industry, was also a hub for Christian workers. With the ever-expanding horizons in travel, evangelists and missionaries could more easily visit other lands and those from across the ocean could visit Chicago.

One such traveler was Dwight L. Moody whose ministry took him to the British Isles and beyond, always accompanied by his song leader, Ira Sankey. The sales from Ira B. Sankey's *1001 Best Songs* alone brought in more than a million dollars. With these funds Moody started his Bible institute and built a large red brick church on the corner of LaSalle and Chicago Avenues.

Great crowds were attracted to Moody's preaching. He was a common man but greatly gifted by God. Churches in Chicago longed for supernatural visitations of God such as Moody had experienced overseas.

"What we need are all-night prayer meetings so that revival will come to our churches," pastors pleaded from pulpits across the city. "Let's pray that God will send a Welsh evangelist to Chicago."

Many a night Anna Louise Jacobson joined others for prayer in the large rented auditorium, her children, Anna and Gerhard, covered with blankets and sleeping on the bench beside her. By dawn the meeting broke up and, tired but rejoicing, the people went back to their homes.

Years passed before Emmanuel Jones from Wales responded to the call from the Chicago churches to be their evangelist. He was short with dark curly hair. His fiery speech and manner impressed the thousands who gathered to hear him.

One special night the seats were filling fast as Mother Anna Louise and Gerhard, now seventeen years old, searched out a place in the front row. The air was filled with a marked expectancy as the people gathered. Hymns rang out with great intensity and fervency. A solemn hush filled the auditorium after the opening prayer as Evangelist Jones stepped into the pulpit, his clear deep voice reverberating through the building, his deep-set eyes penetrating every soul.

"There is a way which seemeth right unto a man, but the end thereof are the ways of death" (Proverbs 14:12, KJV) was his text. People and scenes sprang to life as he preached. Tonight the picture was of a beautiful but floundering ship in a storm.

Anna and Gerhard sat transfixed as the speaker described a life without God—no goal, no chart, no captain's hand to steer—yes, a beautiful life perhaps, but with no future. Choosing one's own way was like that ship headed for destruction.

"Tonight every young person who has never asked the Lord Jesus Christ to be the Captain of your life is following your own way. You are sinking. Perhaps all the years of the future are wrapped up in your decision tonight. What will it be?"

Young Gerhard's heart was beating wildly. His hands gripped the seat in front of him. *Some other night,* a voice said inside, *not tonight.*

But, deep within, Gerhard knew it must be tonight. Yet it was so hard to leave his seat. His mother touched his arm and motioned him to go forward with her. That was all he needed. Trembling, he followed.

At the front someone was singing, "Softly and tenderly Jesus is calling." The altar was full and still streams of people were pouring down the aisles. After Gerhard had wept and confessed his stubbornness and pride, someone knelt beside him and helped him read Bible verses that gave him the assurance that God had heard his prayer and had received him as His child. The atmosphere seemed charged with joy.

Gerhard rose from his knees and, with a glory on his face, gave his first stumbling testimony. All the way home on the late-night streetcar, songs of praise rang out from passengers who had attended the meetings.

In the days that followed, Gerhard realized that a great change had taken place in his life and in the lives of his younger brother and sisters. He thought about the "set of the sail" of his life. In a few months he would graduate from high school. At seventeen it was not too early to ask the Lord to direct him. He had promised his father he would attend business college. But what did God want him to do?

4

Matching Pearls: Two People, One Prayer

A cruel wind blew down Clark Street from Lake Michigan. Among the few streetcar passengers struggling against the sleet and snow was a tall, thin figure pushing his way to the white clapboard house on Clifton Avenue.

"Almost there," he said, mumbling into his woolen scarf and wrenching the door open with the last of his remaining strength.

Taking one look at her husband stumbling through the door, Anna Louise cried, "Oh, John, are you sick? You've been working too many hours at the shop. I've warned you about that. Please, let me help you to the chair."

"Never mind, I can get up. I'm just tired," John murmured.

Later that night John developed a fever and lay sick for days. At last he consented to be seen by the family doctor.

"What is the matter with him, doctor?" Anna Louise wanted to know. "He doesn't seem very sick except that he gets weaker every day."

Dr. Anderson took off his thick glasses and ran his fingers through his hair. Putting his hand under the woman's elbow, the doctor led her to the living room.

"Your husband has acute anemia. There is little we know to do that will help him recover, but I'm sure that with a better diet he will improve. And . . . well . . . who knows. . . ." He shrugged his shoulders, then smiled. "I may be wrong. He probably will live to be old and gray like me."

Father John slowly improved. One day as Gerhard brought him his supper and medicine, he grumbled, "Why don't you ever sit down, Gay? I don't get to talk with you these days. You're always in a hurry."

"Ya, Pa? I'll sit here on your bed. I'm not in a hurry tonight."

"Listen, Gay, I have been thinking," John said reflectively. "You have finished your business course and now are working. Does that brush company pay you enough?"

"I like it for the time being," replied Gerhard.

"For the time being?"

"Ya, Pa. But you know, I told you, since those missionaries from China were in our home I haven't felt content to spend the rest of my life here in America. I feel God wants me to be a pastor or a missionary." Gerhard spoke tentatively, his eyes reading his father's face.

The once ambitious man sank back onto his pillow.

"Ya, I know, but what if something happens to your Pa? Albert doesn't have a good job. Dave is traveling for his company. Someone will have to take care of your mother and sisters in the future." Father John had slipped back into his beloved Swedish.

"Even if you aren't well now, you will be," Gerhard assured his father. "We will always have the rent from the apartments too, Pa." Gerhard squeezed his father's hand goodbye and made a dash for the door where his sister Anna was waiting impatiently. They were already late for the youth meeting at the Moody Church. The group had grown steadily under the leadership of these two dedicated young people.

With these duties and the many others at the Moody Church connected with Christian Endeavor, Gerhard began to sense the need for training. He could see himself standing in a pulpit preaching after he graduated from Moody, but for now, he would have to find another job in or near the institute to help himself through school. When an opening for bookkeeper came up, Gerhard got the job.

After supper that evening, the family sat around the table talking about how the Lord was leading in each of their lives. Father John beamed appreciatively and Mother Anna Louise clapped with joy. Her Gay was to be studying at the institute. Yes, she could imagine him as a pastor some day.

By 1914 there was war in Europe but as yet it had little effect on ordinary people in the United States. Nevertheless, German subs were prowling the high seas. Gerhard put away the newspaper and adjusted the black patch on his eye. Working at the Moody Institute in a dimly lit room had affected his already weak eyes and Chicago's harsh winters had certainly not helped his lungs.

However, today his thoughts were on the Christian Endeavor's annual Valentine banquet. Previously he had always taken his sister Anna, but recently he had been thinking about a certain petite, dark-haired girl. He knew her as one of three sisters who lived at the Chicago Hebrew Mission with their mother. How would Anna feel if he asked Alma Amstutz to the banquet?

Gerhard finally got up his courage and asked his sister if he could bring a young lady for his date instead of her.

"No, I'll not let you—unless the girl is the one I have in mind," Anna replied, cocking her head with a mischievous smile.

"Well, what do you think of Alma Amstutz?" Gerhard's eyes twinkled.

"I knew she was the one! I think she is perfect for you. Every time we have a testimony meeting she is one of the first to jump to her feet. There is nothing artificial about her Christian life."

Two things about that first date with Alma stood out in Gerhard's memory for years to come—the deep, pure joy of fellowship centered in the Lord Jesus Christ and the ride home. He often recalled their happy conversation and how, as they neared the Chicago Hebrew Mission, Alma had turned her face toward him.

"Gerhard," she began nervously, "I'm going to be a missionary to China. I am not interested in a serious friendship with anyone who does not have the same goal in life as mine."

There was an awkward silence as Gerhard stumbled for words.

Finally he said, "Well, I have been praying for China too. On the walls of my bedroom you will see the ones I pray for. Let's go on being friends and trust the Lord to lead us."

That evening Alma Amstutz prayed that God would direct this new-found friendship with Gerhard Jacobson. Even as she prayed, there was someone else praying just as fervently in another part of the city. "Lord, You know for a long long time I've been asking You for a consecrated missionary-minded wife. Please let

Alma love me if You have chosen us for each other."

Spring is a time for rejoicing even in Chicago—housewives cleaning windows and airing winter clothes before storing them away; and tulips and daffodils blooming in small, windswept yards. But the home at 3045 Clifton was not happy. Father Jacobson had sold his tailor shop and was no longer able to go to work. Dread filled the heart of each family member as they visited the room off the front parlor. Gerhard too spent every possible moment after work with his father.

"Gay," John whispered one afternoon, "the Lord is good to give me a son who will preach." He paused and gave Gerhard's hand a firm squeeze. "Your grandparents in Sweden would have been so happy. You will take care of the family when I'm gone, won't you?" A worried crease furrowed his brow.

"Pa, we love you. Don't talk like that," Gerhard said, choking back his tears.

"That's all I can say now, son. I'm tired. I'm going to sleep." Father John turned away and Gerhard tiptoed out of the room.

After supper that evening when Anna Louise entered with her husband's medicine, there was no response from the form on the bed. Setting down the tray, she put her hand on John's cheek. He did not stir. John Jacobson had slipped away to his Savior.

One Friday evening several weeks later, Gerhard wondered if Alma would invite him home after the meeting. She looked especially lovely in a blue suit with matching hat.

"Gay, come to the house after the service," Alma finally said. "I baked a pie—your favorite. There is something I want to ask you."

"Is the pie lemon with meringue?" Gerhard asked as he bent down to look into her deep blue eyes. It was always fun to tease each other as they rode home to the Hebrew Mission. Gerhard enjoyed Alma's sisters and admired Mother Sarah. In many ways she seemed like a young person. She sang around the house, made her guests feel at home and lent an atmosphere of joy wherever she was.

"What did you want to talk to me about, Alma?" Gay finally asked.

Alma's eyes sparkled.

"Mrs. Rounds was here today and told us that we need someone to clean up the Center at the Hebrew Mission after our children's classes and to wash those horribly big windows. She also thinks that a young man could handle the boys better than we ladies do. Would you like to pray about taking the job? There is a small salary connected with it."

And so Gerhard Jacobson became a full-time employee of the Hebrew Mission. The best part about it was that it put him in close proximity to the attractive Alma.

5

Matched Pearls: The Decision

September, month of golden days, flaming leaves and cool nights, swept across the Midwest. This was also the month of holy days for Jews. The first was Rosh Hashannah, the Jewish New Year. Ten days later was Yom Kippur or Day of Atonement, followed by Sukkot, the Feast of Tabernacles. These celebrations provided the workers of the Hebrew Mission with wonderful opportunities for ministry as Jewish acquaintances held open house for friends and relatives.

In the Mission auditorium, Alma and Rhoda Amstutz set up tables for the girls' sewing class. And, outside in the vacant lot, the boys were whooping and hollering at a game of basketball.

As the big bell rang, the girls put their things

away and the boys trooped into the hall with Gerhard, tired and disheveled, bringing up the rear. It was story time.

"Today, your parents will remind you of the story of Abraham and how he was willing to offer his only son as a sacrifice in obedience to God," Alma began. "But God provided a ram as a sacrifice instead. This story is a picture of how God, the heavenly Father, offered His Son Jesus Christ as a sacrifice for the sins of the world. How we should love and thank Jesus for that!

"At Yom Kippur," she continued, "you will remember the story of the lamb that Aaron the priest sacrificed for the sins of the Jewish nation. That pure little lamb is another wonderful picture of Jesus who died for the sins of the whole world."

Alma continued her story, generously sprinkling it with Yiddish expressions. There were tears in many eyes as she closed with an invitation to receive Christ. The open response was more than Gerhard, Alma or Rhoda expected.

"I wonder what will happen when the parents hear about this," Rhoda wondered aloud. The young people were soon to find out.

The following Saturday, Gerhard, dressed in faded work clothes, ragged shoes and a red bandana around his forehead, arrived to do his usual janitorial work at the Mission. He got out his ladder and was preparing to wash "those horribly long windows" as Alma called them. He had just climbed to the top of the ladder and was sloshing water on the first window when he heard a shout from the street.

"Hey, you up there! Come down, will ya?"

Below him Gerhard could see several large Irish policemen. *What's going on?* he wondered to himself. *Maybe some of the Jewish kids are in trouble with the police.* Slowly climbing down the shaky ladder, Gerhard faced the officers.

"Say, fella, we heard there's a reverend around here and he's been trying to change the religion of the kids." The biggest officer glared at Gerhard. "Do you know where we can find him? The chief at the station wants to talk with him."

Boy, am I in trouble, Gerhard thought. *The Jews are stirred up because of the last Bible class.*

"Well, gentlemen," Gerhard finally responded, starting up the ladder, "look the place over. Is there anyone around here that looks like a reverend?"

"You're the only man around the place today?" the second officer asked.

"Yes, I am, and I hope you'll allow me to continue my work." Safely out of reach at the top of the ladder, Gerhard waved the policemen a cheery goodbye.

"Wait 'til I tell the Amstutz ladies about this!" Gerhard grinned, thinking about how he'd mimic the policemens' accents and conversation.

He finished the window washing and headed to the Amstutz apartment. It would feel good to get cleaned up and besides, he could hardly wait to tell them about the visit.

After they had all had a good laugh, a more somber thought penetrated their minds: How would this affect future ministry to these Jewish young people?

One evening, a year later, Gerhard arrived at the Hebrew Mission. As usual, the Amstutz family greeted him warmly. He presented Sarah, by now his mother-in-law-to-be, a big bouquet of flowers from his mother's garden.

"Mother," he asked, "is it OK for me to take Alma to my favorite Swedish restaurant?"

"Ya, that sounds good," Sarah responded happily.

Swanson's Coffee House was crowded as Gerhard and Alma found their way to a cozy corner table. Gerhard's face was glowing, his speech barely above a whisper.

"Honey," he said nervously, "I think we should get married immediately. We won't have a wedding at the Moody Church nor even a public one. We will just save the money for the things we need for China. What do you say?"

Tears clouded Alma's eyes.

"I've been so tired since I've been working at the hospital and studying too," she replied. "I'll be glad to have it simple, darling. Do you have any ideas?"

"Well, you have some Alliance friends on the southside, don't you?" Gerhard asked.

"You mean Rev. Wester? Yes, they're Mother's friends and mine too."

"Well, what do you think about the 18th? Does that date suit you? Our apartment is nearly ready. We'll get the couch and easy chair you like so much and I'm having a rug delivered tomorrow." Gerhard's dimples flashed in and out as he spoke.

The decision was made.

August the 18th dawned in cloudless brilliance. Going to her closet, Alma took down the pink silk going-away dress she had made. *It looks good on me even if I do say so myself,* Alma thought as she caught a glimpse of herself in the mirror. Because this was such a special day, she took a little extra time with her hair. Finally, with a quick glance back at her room, she picked up her purse and stepped out into the hallway.

"Isn't that a pretty fancy dress just for going out with Gay?" Rhoda asked as Alma appeared.

"Oh, you know," the secret bride-to-be began slowly, "we are visiting some special friends on the southside." There was an awkward pause. "It's a nice cool dress for a hot day," she finished lamely.

Calling a cheery "goodbye," she ran down the stairs to the reading room where Gay was waiting. *He is so handsome*, she murmured to herself as his smile greeted her around the corner.

"I thought I'd wait and see the color of your

dress before I bought roses for the wedding," he said sheepishly.

Hand in hand the couple filled the time on the train talking about the new life before them. At the flower shop Gay bought two dozen pink roses. It was more than Alma felt appropriate.

A carriage took them to the home of Rev. Wester where their vows were made before God and man. The evening ended around a specially decorated table filled with food lovingly prepared for the newlyweds by Mrs. Wester.

And then it was time to go home.

"Now for the worst," Alma giggled as they pushed open the Mission door and tiptoed inside. "We have to tell everyone."

Sarah Amstutz was disappointed at the elopement, as was Anna Jacobson, but at each home there were belated parties and showers. Everything the couple needed for their home was supplied.

Within weeks, word came that Nellie Bowen had died of smallpox complications at the mountain resort of Jigonshan (Gee gung SHAN), China. Alma was heartbroken.

"Oh, Lord," she cried, "Gerhard and I will take her place. Just lead us to China."

But with no doors opening for the anxious couple, just how and when was the question.

6

Prepared Pearls: China at Last!

The passports were in hand and the Grace Mission brochures printed and mailed to friends. The Grace Mission, Gerhard had taken care to explain, came into existence through the efforts of the Rev. and Mrs. Alexander Kennedy, missionaries to China.

Founded in 1889, the work had grown from one large church in the city of Dongxi (DONG see) to include a number of outstations. Those outstations now needed a couple to spearhead a training program for lay pastors to support and follow up the evangelism ministry of Rev. Kennedy. It seemed to be just the kind of work Gerhard and Alma were fitted to do.

The days were filled with the rush of farewell meetings, the most impressive being the service at the Moody Memorial Church where Gerhard and Alma had served so faithfully.

The elders and deacons, as well as Pastors Paul Rader and E.Y. Woolley, officiated at the service. As the young couple were commissioned for missionary work and Dr. Rader offered the prayer of dedication, there was hardly a dry eye in the church.

Many in the congregation wondered if they would ever see the Jacobsons again. Other Americans had already succumbed to the fearful Chinese scourges of cholera, dysentery, smallpox or typhoid. What would be the future of this frail couple who both appeared so small and weak? But had not the Scripture said, "God chose the weak things of the world to shame the strong" (1 Corinthians 1:27)?

So it was that in February 1918, Gerhard and Alma Jacobson left Chicago enroute to China. The "matched pearls" were now polished and ready. But would the polish provide what they needed when confronted by the enemy in the Land of the Dragon?

Thursday evening. Alma was whirling around the room, holding nine-month-old Doris.

"To China we will go, To China we will go,
  Hi-o the dairi-o, To China we will go."

The final rush to make the train for the first leg of their long journey to China would be hectic for Alma and Gerhard. Mother Jacobson nestled Doris in her ample bosom as she quietly hummed a Swedish lullaby. Wiping her tears away, she wondered when she would see this chubby little granddaughter again. A missionary's seven-year term on the field was a long time. It would bring great changes in everyone's life.

Just then the doorbell rang and footsteps were heard on the stairs. The door flung open as friends from the Chicago Hebrew Mission pushed into the room.

"Here, take these flowers for your trip," Mrs. Olson said, thrusting a fragrant bouquet of assorted blooms into Alma's hand.

Mr. Olson and Gerhard carried the baggage down to the waiting car. Mother Jacobson did not feel up to the strain of going to the station—those farewells had been said earlier. But Mother Sarah Amstutz arrived with the other workers. Those who could not fit into the car went on the streetcar to Chicago's Union Station.

It was dark as the Model-T Ford threaded its way along Chicago's dimly lit streets. Questions without answers raced through the young missionaries' minds. Feelings of excitement and sorrow clamored for supremacy. Then, before they knew it, the glass-canopied station came into view.

"Here they come," shouted a crowd at the sidewalk as the familiar car approached. Soon

Gerhard and Alma and baby Doris were surrounded by the triumphant but melancholy strains of "God Be with You Till We Meet Again." Many in the group could hardly finish as they choked with emotion. Everyone stretched out their hands for a last touch of the dearly loved couple.

Then, slowly, with great clouds of steam and slow-heaving chugs, the train backed out of the station. With tears streaming down their faces, Gerhard and Alma watched until the flutter of hands and handkerchiefs vanished from sight. What would China be like?

Up ahead the skyline of the city of Shanghai pierced the horizon. Gay rushed to see if Alma had finished tidying up the cabin before docking. *This will be our first glimpse of China and I don't want her to miss it,* he thought to himself as he hurried down the passageway. Soon the family joined other wide-eyed passengers at the rails.

The harbor was crowded. Battleships from various nations lay at anchor in the river. Junks plowed by with sails aflutter in the morning breeze. Tiny sampans with laundry flapping from bamboo poles glided past the giant liner. And in the background they could see Shanghai's skyscrapers dwarfing the throngs of people in the streets.

Moments later the ship nudged the dockside and the passengers crowded to the gangplank eager to get their landlegs back again. It had been twenty-one days since they had boarded the ship *Empress of Asia* in Vancouver, Canada. With Gerhard and Alma was Emma Sweet, a missionary returning to her post in China.

"Never mind, folks," said Mrs. Sweet as they bemoaned the fact that Alexander Kennedy of the Grace Mission had failed to appear. "I'll hire carriers to take our things to the Dearborn Sisters' Shanghai Guest Home."

Several days went by before the anticipated letter from Mr. Kennedy arrived. It informed the Jacobsons that after passing customs and paying their respects to the American Consul they were to wire the time of their arrival in Hangzhou (Hahng JO). Alexander Kennedy would meet them there and take them by houseboat up the Grand Canal to Dongxi.

Their brief glimpses of Shanghai with its millions stirred them to the depths. Beggars flooded the streets, some with self-inflicted wounds designed to arouse sympathy. Sick people were left in the open to die. Unwanted baby girls were flung into the river. *How could God's light shine in the midst of such darkness in this Land of the Dragon?* Gerhard wondered.

It was a relief to reach Hangzhou and find their way by rickshaw to Mrs. Sweet's home, a tall, well-built house with wide verandas encircling it. Here everything made one feel one was back home in the United States. "A kind of bittersweet sentiment," Alma sighed.

"I thought this is where we are supposed to meet Mr. Kennedy," Gay finally said as Emma Sweet served them tea and cookies. "I wonder where he is?" He did not have long to wait for the answer to his question.

At breakfast the next morning, there sat Mr. Kennedy. He didn't look at all like his picture. He was a short, thin man with slightly graying dark hair and deep-set blue eyes.

"I have two boats hired to take us to Dongxi," he said finally after the greetings were over. "I think they are waiting for us even now."

The group was carried through the streets in curtained sedan chairs until they reached the Grand Canal. Bobbing in the water below were two boats, one for the baggage, the other for passengers. At the bottom of the steep stone steps, the boatman helped them into the craft and led the way to some benches.

"Everything is provided," Mr. Kennedy explained as they settled into their seats. "In a few moments you'll see the boatman's wife lift up the floorboards, get out her two charcoal stoves and cook vegetables and rice for us."

"Where do they get the water for drinking and cooking?" Alma asked, eyeing the brown, debris-filled canal water in which they were anchored.

"From the canal. But don't worry. It's boiled and considered safe." Mr. Kennedy laughed at the look on Alma's face.

The evening sun was throwing slanting rays across a sky of gold and crimson as the city of Dongxi slowly came into view. This was their destination. This was the city they would call home for, as far as they knew now, the rest of their lives. It had been a long, wearisome trip—from Chicago to Vancouver, then the tedious trip across the Pacific, their arrival in Shanghai, and now the end of the journey to the city that cradled their future.

Gerhard and Alma watched as open-faced shops perched on one side of the canal and houses behind high walls on the opposite side slid by them. At one of them, a crowd of people gathered. As the houseboat dropped anchor, suddenly hundreds of firecrackers exploded into the evening sky, lighting up the street.

"Our people are giving you a royal welcome," explained Mr. Kennedy as the Jacobsons stood wide-eyed.

Baby Doris began to cry. This brought peals of laughter from the crowd. Everyone was calling out greetings and bowing low and repeatedly to the newcomers.

"Just do as they do," Mr. Kennedy advised in English, returning the bows. *So this is the way the Chinese welcome their friends,* thought Alma and Gerhard as they bowed awkwardly.

The huge iron gates groaned as an elderly gatekeeper swung them open and led the way around a large church building to a brick walkway that wound in and out between several smaller buildings. With his key he opened a red-painted gate and let the little family in. A native-style, two-story house planted in the middle of an expansive garden stood directly in front of them. Alma breathed deeply. The scent of roses, lilies and peach blossoms wafted through the air.

Mrs. Kennedy appeared.

"Welcome! Welcome! We've been waiting all day," she said smiling graciously.

Grace Kennedy was a striking-looking woman with brown hair and eyes and a musical voice.

"I hope you'll feel at home with us," she continued. "We feel we know you already from all the letters. Everyone has been eagerly awaiting your arrival. Our house is Chinese and so are our customs. I hope you'll get used to things."

"Oh, this is what we've been looking forward to and we feel at home already," Gerhard responded cheerfully.

"We've waited supper for you," continued Mrs. Kennedy. "Can you come downstairs after a little wash-up? I'll ring a bell."

That night as the Jacobsons had their usual prayer time together before retiring, silent tears began to run down Alma's cheeks.

"Don't tell me you're homesick for your mother again, Alma," Gerhard chided her jokingly.

"No, honey, I'm just so happy. These are tears of joy. I already love the country and the people. China!" she breathed, a deep sigh of contentment escaping her lips. "We're home at last."

7

The Dragon's Claws: A Spiritual Battle

"There are two things we need to take care of today, Brother Jacobson," Mr. Kennedy announced the next morning after a breakfast of eggs and soft boiled rice. Gerhard waited for him to continue.

"We need to take both of you to the shops to buy cloth for Chinese clothes and then to the tailor shop to be measured. You'll also need Chinese cotton shoes."

With breakfast finished, they hurried to a waiting sampan and crossed the canal to the market on the opposite side. Gerhard and Alma panted as they climbed the steep stone steps from the river to the street level.

"Whatever you see, don't act as if you want to buy it or the shopkeeper will raise the price,"

Mr. Kennedy warned. "Just give me a nod and we'll talk price."

Since the cook was along with his market basket, Mr. Kennedy decided to introduce the Jacobsons to the food market. Crude stalls were piled with fruits and vegetables resembling few Gerhard and Alma had ever seen. Meat hung on large hooks gathering flies. Fish flapped on oiled sheets spread on boards. A noisy crowd followed the Americans.

"What are they saying?" Gerhard wanted to know.

"Oh, they're describing our long noses, blue eyes and dry-looking hair," Alexander Kennedy chuckled. "We won't stand out so much when you get your Chinese clothes."

The silk shops were spectacular. The endless brocade patterns, the rainbow colors, the styles of jackets, vests and gowns amazed the newcomers. After their purchase they hurried off to the tailor shop and, by noon, the party was back home.

Both Alma and Gerhard were anxious to begin language study but a good teacher was hard to find. When Mr. Wang (WAHNG) finally arrived, they devoted both morning and afternoon to study. But Gerhard was restless. He was anxious to get out into the villages where the full extent of the Grace Mission's work could be explored.

"Next month," said Mr. Kennedy, "I'll be going for a three-week trip to the outstations and

I'll be glad for you to accompany me and our workers. But tomorrow we must be ready for the local villagers who are preparing a welcome feast for you."

The next day before daylight cracked the morning sky the village cooks were arriving with baskets of meats and vegetables. By midday the guests began to arrive. This, according to Kennedy, was to be a *re lau* (REH LAO) or "hot and noisy affair." The air was electric with excitement.

The dinner which was to have begun at noon finally commenced shortly before 3 o'clock. Gerhard watched as the head deacon fussed over the seating arrangements, making sure to observe strict etiquette. It was important that all the dignitaries face the front door. Those of next importance were to be seated on their right.

The program began when Dr. Wu, a former Confucian scholar dressed in a long, gray-silk gown with a black brocade vest, began his speech. A shiny queue swayed from beneath a satin skull cap with every motion of his arms. With each important statement he would rise on tiptoe and bounce back down with a thud. His clipped tones, though loud and clear, often ended in a squeak.

"We are here to welcome the new missionaries, Pastor and Mrs. Jacobson," he began. "It is through the missionaries that we have learned to love and serve the true God and His Son Jesus Christ.

"Many ask me why China needs to hear about Jesus when we have Confucius. I tell them three things. First, Confucius was a teacher. Jesus is our Savior. China needs a Savior from sin and its guilt.

"Second, Confucius said that there are many ways to heaven and by doing our best we may hope to get there. Jesus said, 'I am the Way,' the only way to our Father in heaven.

"Third, Confucius' tomb can be found today because he is dead. Jesus Christ's tomb is empty because He is alive. He lives and He lives in our hearts. Someday He will come again, our King."

After Dr. Wu's speech others added their words of appreciation for the coming of the new missionaries. Alma and Gerhard understood little of the words, but fully comprehended the warmth of the sentiments.

The rays of the afternoon sun were beginning to slant westward when the toastmaster announced that the "light lunch" was soon to begin. Waiters brought in dishes of cold pork garnished with walnuts, duck wings covered with almonds and mounds of beef cut to chopstick-bite size. All the guests stood by their seats as the blessing was pronounced.

One by one, in lightning succession, eighteen courses were served: fried shrimp, chicken balls in peach sauce, fried cucumber in creamed chicken and boiled pigeons in a large soup tureen, their heads draped over the dish's edge, yellow feet sticking up. There was also Peking duck wrapped in paper-thin pancakes and Yellow River fish complete with heads and tails, whose glassy eyes stared at the celebrants. A sweet dish was served halfway through the meal and more spicy dishes followed. As soon as each dish was placed on the table, the chief guests were served, then others dived in with their chopsticks until it was gone.

After the meal Gerhard gave a response in English which Dr. Wu did his best to interpret. More speeches followed, then the meal ended with bowls of tea. "See you again" and "go slowly" were repeated over and over as the crowd filtered through the big iron gates and into the night.

The day for the visit to the country churches finally arrived. Before daylight the watchman was awakened by a terrible banging at the front gate.

"Open up! Open up!" shouted a voice.

"What is it?" the sleepy gatekeeper called back.

"The wind is up and the boat is ready to leave. Tell the foreign pastors to come immediately."

And so began the long trip to the villages for the Grace Mission director and his junior missionary. In each village where they stopped along the canal, groups of church members awaited them. At times they stayed for several

THE DRAGON'S CLAWS: A SPIRITUAL BATTLE

days, preaching and visiting the people. The love and hospitality of the Christians contrasted sharply with the often-heard slanderous remarks flung at them by others. Some villagers even displayed open hostility to the missionaries.

"Why do they hate us?" Gerhard asked Mr. Kennedy one day as they strolled along a dike.

"Actually, there are many reasons," the senior missionary replied. "I think it began with the days of the Opium Wars when Britain forced opium from India on China to increase her trade. A white face reminds them of that. Then, after the Boxer Rebellion, when foreign lives and foreign property suffered, China was charged millions in indemnity to some Western nations. This seriously crippled their economy. Also, we need to remember that the Chinese are very superstitious. They fear that our teachings of Christianity have offended their pagan deities, the spirits of the land and the air causing plagues, floods and famines throughout the land. Evil spirits are real in this land, brother."

"I've seen many temples and idols but I never thought they had any real power," Gerhard remarked as they passed a wayside shrine where joss sticks burned silently.

"Don't be deceived, Brother Jacobson. We are in a great spiritual battle. The enemy would like to defeat us, even to take our lives if he could. Listen, I hear wailing."

A door in a nearby house opened and a woman's figure could be seen silhouetted against the light. She was shaking a child's garment, calling and crying, "Little spirit, come back, come back."

"Why is she calling for the little spirit to come back?" Gerhard wondered aloud.

"Her child must be sick and she thinks one of his three spirits has wandered away from its body. She fears that if the child becomes worse, the other spirits will leave and her child will die."

That night, after their meeting with the village Christians, it was suggested that a group of them visit the family with the sick child. Making their way through the narrow streets, they finally arrived at the house. As they began to pray, the small boy stirred, his breathing became less labored and the flushed color slowly faded from his cheeks.

"*Ayi yah*, (EYE YAH) the child improves," the mother breathed gratefully. The father stirred up the fire and prepared hot tea for the visitors.

"Pray for my new baby too, even though she's only a girl," the mother requested as she picked up a tiny bundle from a corner of the bed.

"May I see her?" Gerhard asked, gingerly removing the covering. There, tucked in the blanket, was an exquisitely shaped face, soft dark hair, tiny eyelashes and a rosebud mouth.

"She's so lovely, isn't she?" Gerhard exclaimed before he remembered that in Chinese culture it was inappropriate to praise a child before it was a month old. Jealous spirits, they believed, would seek to destroy it.

Fear suddenly crossed the mother's face. Going quickly to her idol shelf, she lit two sticks of incense. As the ascending smoke wrapped itself around the idols, the woman's face relaxed. Now the spirits were surely appeased. Her child would be safe.

"Why are you so afraid?" a motherly Bible woman asked, laying a kindly hand on the woman's shoulder. "You saw how our true God healed your boy in answer to prayer. He is greater than all the evil spirits."

Quietly she began to tell the frightened mother the story of the Great Physician and Savior, Jesus Christ. After a closing prayer, the Christians left.

In the years to come, Gerhard would never forget the wisdom and spiritual insight Alexander Kennedy showed on that trip to the villages, though at the time he scarcely understood the significance of it all.

But God knew.

8

The Dragon's Power: A Tragic Summer, a New Ministry

It was a sparkling spring day, a wonderful respite after days and days of rain.

"This is May and the humid heat is beginning," announced Mrs. Kennedy at the breakfast table one morning. Pausing to sprinkle salt on her papaya, she continued. "The children will be home from the school in Shanghai in another few days and we will soon be starting out for Mokanshan (Mo kan SHAHN) for the summer. The cottage there is large enough for our family and for yours as well."

Turning to her husband, Mrs. Kennedy asked, "But you'll not be staying the whole summer, will you, dear?"

"No," replied Mr. Kennedy, "I plan to stay only long enough to see that you're all settled. Then I'll go to Yunnan (You NAHN) as I did last summer. I think my health is better there."

"What about our language teacher?" asked Gerhard. "Will he go along?"

"No, he'll have to stay with his family, but we can find one up there, I think," Mr. Kennedy responded. As it would turn out, the tragic events of the summer would leave no time for language study. That would have to wait until fall—if funds permitted.

Mokanshan, translated by some as "Don't Worry Mountain," was a favorite summer resort for foreign residents. Although it was only a little over 2,000 feet high, the strong mountain breezes brought a pleasant respite from the hot and humid air of the plains. In 1917 there were 116 foreign residences in Mokanshan with a population of less than 1,000 at the height of the summer season.

A week later the Kennedys and their four children, George and Fred, who were teenagers, and Donald and Grace, younger but noisier, together with the Jacobsons and their servants set out for the resort. The trip began in the evening when the wind was more likely to catch the sails of the boats—the Grace Mission houseboat carrying the Kennedys and the Jacobsons, and the second one, a rice boat, loaded with sixty-five pieces of baggage plus passengers.

While the moon in the eastern sky reflected

the sunset's afterglow, Gerhard reached for some writing paper:

> I can hear the murmuring voices of the boatmen and the gentle splashing of paddles in the dark water. The moon, which has changed colors from pink and lavender to dazzling blue, is reflected by what looks like a wave of diamonds with each stroke of the paddles. Alma is trying to put Doris to sleep under the net.
>
> From a temple the sound of bells and drums makes me shiver. Boatmen on a passing boat are whistling to the wind spirits. The atmosphere is heavy and oppressive on my soul. This is indeed a dark, dark land, the Land of the Dragon, the devil.

About 4 a.m. the next morning the boats docked. Gradually the passengers awoke and assembled their baggage in the gray of the pre-dawn morning. It was a steep and treacherous climb up the bank of the canal to the road above.

"Follow me," the cook shouted. "I think I can find the way to the guest house. Be careful not to slip in the mud."

Dawn was breaking as the sleepy group came upon a squat whitewashed building. A light was shining in the window. Soon they were seated around a rough table having breakfast accompanied by the usual hot tea. Then it was time to head up the mountain.

The first order of business was to haggle with the carriers for the right price. Once that was established, each carrier shouldered his share of the boxes and suitcases—100-200 pounds. Muscles gleamed like molten bronze in the sunlight as they climbed the mountain, their cargo swaying precariously from carrying poles. It was a stiff, eight-hour hike of more than 2,000 feet through the clouds to the top of Mokanshan.

"This is our business section, called the Gap," explained young Fred Kennedy as the road widened at the top of the path and stores appeared on both sides. Fred, a gangly teenager with sandy-colored hair, freckles and bright blue eyes, was both a tireless hiker and talker, switching effortlessly from English to Chinese.

"Look up there to the west of that ridge," he continued. "That brown rock house in ours."

Everyone was relieved to settle into the place that would be their residence for the next several months. The only exception was Mr. Kennedy who left the mountain a few days later for Yunnan.

One day several weeks later, Mrs. Kennedy called Gerhard aside.

"I have a strong feeling that I believe is from the Lord," she confided. "I believe God wants me to go and be with my husband. You and your family are to stay here on the mountain." The four Kennedy children, she added, would also stay on the mountain under the Jacobson's care. It was a strange and unexpected turn of events for Gerhard and Alma.

A month later Mrs. Kennedy wrote from Yunnan requesting prayer for her husband—he was not doing well physically. Alma and Gerhard organized a day of prayer among the dozens of missionaries who were also escaping the heat on the mountain. Nevertheless, a haunting fear plagued Gerhard as he recalled the fever, the night sweats and the cough Mr. Kennedy had experienced on their recent trip to the villages.

That night as Alma and Gerhard were having their evening prayers together, Alma said, "You know, Gay, for some strange reason this verse really struck me during my reading today. It says, 'What I do you know not now, but you shall know hereafter' " (John 13:7). She paused a moment, then began to pray. "Lord," she said, "whatever is ahead for us, give us the grace to face it bravely."

The next day dawned as usual and everyone appeared at the breakfast table except young Fred. He was sick. The Mission doctor feared Fred had cholera as he was vomiting constantly. But later that morning it was revealed that Fred had found some berries on a hike the previous day and had eaten them despite warnings from his companions.

The days that followed only brought intense fever and weakness and more nausea. Alma and Gerhard, along with the other Kennedy children, took turns watching at Fred's bedside day and night.

One afternoon, Fred called Alma to his side.

"I have a message for my mother and dad," he whispered softly as Alma cradled his hand in hers. "Tell them I love them and I love Jesus."

It was August 13. Wild winds were whipping the gray clouds and moaning around the little mountain cottage. Alma stayed with Fred from 2 o'clock in the morning until 4 when Gerhard came to spell her off. Exhausted, she had no sooner crept into bed than her husband called to her.

Neither could hold back the tears as they huddled together by Fred's bed. They were still there when the morning sun broke through the mist, shedding a soft glow over the room. Suddenly, Fred's eyes opened and a faint smile crossed his lips. His eyes swept the faces around him. Then they clouded over and closed. His body gave a great shudder. He was gone.

The days seemed to tumble together. Gerhard left for Dongxi to prepare for the burial. Meanwhile, Alma arranged for Fred's funeral to be held at 3 o'clock the afternoon of the day he passed away. The church was packed, the altar adorned with lovingly made wreaths and other flower arrangements.

Fred's casket was placed in a sturdy wooden box for the trip to Dongxi and burial in the Chinese Christian cemetery. It would be a month before the Kennedys would receive the news of his death. They had scarcely known he was even sick.

Then, shock of all shocks: A messenger came to the mountain with the news that Mr. Kennedy had also gone to be with Jesus. He died September 2. Mrs. Kennedy had still not heard the news of Fred's death when she sent the telegram.

That evening as Gerhard lay in bed he thought, *The Dragon seems so powerful in China. He has unexpectedly snatched away two lives.* Then another thought overshadowed the first. It was a comforting thought: *God knows the length of our days. He holds the key to the future and the enemy is not more powerful than our God.*

Ah, yes, the future. The future was now Gerhard's major concern. What did the future hold for him and Alma and for Grace Mission now that Alexander Kennedy was gone?

The Jacobsons had been in China for six months and their ocean freight had just arrived in Shanghai. It was, they were told, even now on its way to Dongxi. But today was Thursday, September 28. In just four days the Jacobsons would leave for Nanking Language School to complete their language study. What a mad scramble it would be for them to repack and get ready for their nine months in Nanking.

November 11, 1918 was a crisp, cool day in Nanking, a day seemingly just like any other day. But it would be a day the world would never forget. In the middle of the morning the cannon at the Drum Tower began to boom across the city. Guns fired, gongs pounded, church bells rang and firecrackers could be heard everywhere. On the street below, newsboys held up papers announcing that the war was over. The German Kaiser had abdicated and fled to the Netherlands. Peace had come again.

The passing weeks and months seemed like days as Gerhard and Alma concentrated on their studies. And before they knew it, they had passed their exams and were on their way back to Dongxi—and an unknown future.

It was May and the Jacobsons, along with Mrs. Kennedy and her children, were once again nestled within the enfolding arms of "Don't Worry Mountain." This year mist, rains and tropical storms had drenched the mountain ranges, covering them with a verdant gown.

One evening, when the Kennedy children and Doris were especially noisy at the table, Mrs. Kennedy asked Alma, "Have you thought about my suggestion of inviting a young woman from the States to help with caring for your children?"

Alma's blue eyes lit up.

"Yes, we have. My mother's work with the Jews in Chicago is finished and my sister has left for Congo. That means Mother could come to China if the Lord opens the door."

Grace Kennedy's eyes fell.

"I hope you realize that she must be accepted by Moody Church to be a worker."

"Actually, Mother will not be coming out under Moody Church. She will be coming on her own to be with our family," Alma replied, exchanging an "it's already looked after" glance with her husband.

"Well, we'll see about that," Mrs. Kennedy responded curtly, picking up a letter in front of her. "I just received a letter from the church that a Miss Gertrude Bjork hopes to join us in November. It says you know her."

"Oh, yes! We know her personally," Gerhard said, swallowing a mouthful of hot tea.

"It would be helpful if Mother and Gertrude could travel together, wouldn't it?" Alma added as she offered another spoonful of pudding to Doris.

In September, word came that Sarah Amstutz and Gertrude Bjork had boarded the *Isama Maru*, a Japanese ocean liner full of Chinese laborers returning from World War I. The timing couldn't have been better. Alma was expecting her second child. Her mother would arrive just in time to take over the household duties.

Gradually subtle changes began to take place in the Grace Mission. For the Jacobsons the joy of teaching and preaching was fading. Mrs. Kennedy placed Chinese workers, trained and untrained, in positions of responsibility while Gerhard was asked only to supervise the Mission compound. Alma and Gerhard often sat in the church on Sundays wondering why they had come to China. The more they fasted and prayed over the matter, the more one thing became clear: A change was inevitable.

But there were other problems in Dongxi. Idol worship was increasing. The elders of the city, perplexed over the increasing number of epidemics and deaths following the devastating summer floods, decided to have a dragon parade. Appease the gods—that was the answer to the dilemma.

In the midst of this demon worship, Mr. Wu, the evangelist, had an idea.

"Sen Mushe (Sen MOO suh)," he said, calling Gerhard by his Chinese name, "why don't we stand outside the gospel hall as the crowd passes? We can hold up a banner, sing and pass out tracts."

"Good idea," Gerhard replied, "if you think they won't attack us."

It was late in the afternoon when the familiar city streets became strangely quiet. People stood expectantly in their doorways. The parade was about to begin. Suddenly a wild, ear-splitting sound shattered the stillness as temple bells boomed, cymbals crashed and two-stringed violins began to whine.

In the distance a red silk and gold paper dragon appeared. Underneath were men supporting it with poles. It danced, leaped, shook and slithered down the crowded streets, its fiery red mouth spewing out clouds of smoke and flame. There was a savage fascination in the rolling of its eyes and long sweeping tongue. Behind the dragon were men dressed like hideous animals or painted like demons. Brandishing long knives or daggers, they chanted in a high falsetto to the rhythm of the drums. On and on it came. Now it was approaching the chapel.

Gerhard felt a sudden urge to rush inside to avoid a confrontation. He looked at Pastor Wu. His eyes were closed, his lips moving in prayer. Suddenly a man in the parade caught sight of the banner with the name "Jesus" painted on it. He fell to the ground and screamed in terror. The power of God had collided with the power of the dragon.

It was late in the afternoon of the next day before Gerhard and Alma got their first glimpse of the *Isama Maru*.

"There they are, Gay," Alma called out excitedly. "Mother has her same dark blue felt hat and coat."

Sarah Amstutz was waving at the sea of faces on the pier, sure that somewhere in that throng her loved ones were also waving at her. The gangplank had hardly touched the dock when crowds of shouting coolies pushed their way on board. Gerhard followed the two he had hired, with Alma trying to keep up through the crush of bodies.

Tears of joy and laughter bridged the months of separation as mother and daughter embraced.

"I'm so happy to be here," Sarah sobbed. "When I stood up at Paul Rader's missionary meetings, I never thought that someday the Lord would take me at my word and send me to China! It's so good to be here."

Gerhard and Alma were happy she was there, too, for on January 6, about 4 o'clock in the afternoon, tiny Sarah Winifred Jacobson made her appearance.

"I thought all babies were ugly and red," Gerhard remarked as he placed the white-blanketed bundle close to Alma for her first glimpse. "But this one is quite pretty!"

"I'm glad you think so, dear," Alma whispered weakly.

It had been two years since the Jacobsons arrived in China to begin their missionary work with the Grace Mission. After Mr. Kennedy's death, Gerhard and Alma had many talks with Mrs. Kennedy about their desire to be in a pioneer ministry. But clearly, the few counties allotted to the Grace Mission precluded this possibility. Their future with the Mission seemed tenuous at best.

About this time, a copy of *The Alliance Weekly*, a missionary journal of The Christian and Missionary Alliance, arrived. It stated that the Alliance was looking for young couples who would be willing to open stations in the western province of Hunan (HOO nahn) and the southern part of the province of Anhui (AHN whay). Pioneer ministry! That's just what the Jacobsons were looking for. They decided to apply to The Christian and Missionary Alliance and to the China Inland Mission.

"Wouldn't it be something if both the Alliance and the China Inland Mission would accept us here in China but at home in the States they wouldn't?" Alma remarked one evening as together they recalled the traumatic days in Chicago when they had been turned down by both Missions.

"Yes. I believe our dream of a pioneer ministry is unfolding," Gerhard said, folding his arms behind his head and leaning back. "But we don't want to leave Mrs. Kennedy and the Grace Mission without their blessing." Understandably, it was important to Gerhard that the transfer be done in a cordial fashion. But was it possible?

A week later Gerhard was standing on the deck of the river steamer *Jardine Matteson* as it approached Anking (Ahn KING). In the distance he could see a straight road leading from the dock to a massive opening in the city wall about a mile away. From the black-tiled rooftops a broken line of mountains lifted giant shoulders to the morning sky. In a flash the ship's cables hit the dock and a tall Britisher boarded the ship and introduced himself to Gerhard.

"Brother Jacobson, I'm Rev. Young from the China Inland Mission. My wife has a hot meal ready," he said graciously. "We can get acquainted as we ride into the city in my carriage."

Gerhard had come to tour some of the interior cities as a trial run for possible future ministry. But God had other plans. Rains poured down night and day for three days. Cities and villages throughout the region were inundated, making travel impossible. It was disappointing—and perturbing.

On the third day, as Gerhard sat in a cold and dismal room, a knock came at the door. Mr. Young handed him a letter. It was postmarked at Wuchang (Woo CHANG), headquarters of The Christian and Missionary Alliance. The members of the Central China Committee were having a meeting, the letter said, and they had learned that the Jacobsons were interested in pioneer ministry. The Mission was in need of a couple who would venture into South Anhui. Would Mr. Jacobson come immediately for an interview?

Gerhard left Anking sensing that God had closed the door for ministry with the China Inland Mission. His next stop would be the home of Grace Kennedy. His purpose? To resign from the Grace Mission.

Mrs. Kennedy greeted Gerhard cordially. Nervously he explained what he and Alma thought to be God's leading in their lives. Mrs. Kennedy listened intently and seemed reluctant for the Jacobsons to leave the Mission. After a lengthy conversation, Mrs. Kennedy said tearfully, "I want you to know that I respect your decision. Go, and the Lord bless you. We shall all miss you greatly."

Gerhard breathed an inaudible sigh of relief. Then, thanking Mrs. Kennedy for her kindness, he stood and turned to go.

"Wait," interrupted Mrs. Kennedy, "I have something to give you."

She went to her office and returned with a small box in her hand. On the top of the box were the words, "The Anhui Fund." Opening the lid, she removed a large roll of bills.

"This money has come from several sources and was awaiting your decision about staying or going," she said solemnly, handing the roll of bills to Gerhard.

Anhui—and The Christian and Missionary Alliance—it would be!

9

The Dragon's Lair: Datong

Anhui, according to Chinese legend, is a land of extremes, the meeting of north and south, a land of the camel and the buffalo, of wheat and rice, of mountains and plains.

The city of Datong and its environs, spread out on the fertile Yangtze River plain, would provide just the kind of ministry that Gerhard and Alma and The Christian and Missionary Alliance had hoped and prayed for—an open door for village evangelism, plus lay pastor training.

Against the glistening walls of the newly whitewashed chapel dark shadows swayed back and forth to the rhythm of the chorus:

> Jesus breaks every fetter,
> Jesus breaks every fetter,
> Jesus breaks every fetter,
> And He sets me free.

It was the last service on a busy Sunday. Gerhard was still combing his hair in the upstairs bedroom of the Mission house. Reflected in the mirror were the lights from junks gliding down the Yangtze. As Gerhard looped the cloth buttons of his padded silk gown he reminisced. It had been two years since his family had moved into this largest missionary residence in the province of Anhui. Because it provided a stopover for missionaries from the interior, the Jacobsons were hardly ever without visitors.

The compound and school faced the street, as well as residences for teachers, the evangelist's family, the Bible woman and others. In the back stood the Jacobson residence complete with an expansive front lawn, a garden, fruit trees and an abundance of flowers.

Gerhard slipped into the church just as the singing came to an end. Although tired from a long day of ministry, he still preached with freedom and earnestness. The upturned faces of the audience drank in every word as the missionary told of the miracle-working Jesus Christ and His great love and power to change lives.

"You have heard how Jesus healed the sick,

opened the eyes of the blind and brought hope to the hopeless," his voice rang out. "Now wouldn't you like to trust Him as your Savior? He can do the same for you. Come, kneel here at the front and we will pray for you."

At the back of the room a man stood up and cried in a trembling voice, "What can your foreign Jesus do for me, an opium devil for more than thirty years?"

An audible gasp rose from the congregation and everyone turned around. There stood a hollow-eyed creature, his clothing filthy and disheveled.

A hush fell as Gerhard stepped to the railing of the platform and beckoned to the man.

"Come. Jesus came to heal your body and deliver your soul from the bondage of the opium habit," he assured the inquirer.

Hesitantly the man stepped into the aisle.

"How can He do that?" he persisted.

"The missionary doctors, God's servants at the Wuhu (WOO Hoo) hospital, can cure you or you can stay here with us at the Mission compound and we will pray for you. This way is harder and you will suffer greatly, but Jesus alone will heal you."

By now the front of the chapel was filled with men and women seeking the Lord. Gerhard's heart was rejoicing. Pastor Hu and the other Christian workers had been praying for such a break among Christians and unbelievers.

"I will return tomorrow morning and give you my decision," the man promised as he crept away into the night.

"That is what they all say, but don't believe him," Pastor Hu warned Gerhard.

The next morning Gerhard headed to the church early. He had not been in his study long when he was roused from his knees by a sharp rap on the door.

"Sen Mushe, you have visitors," Wang the gatekeeper, called out. Opening the door Gerhard was surprised to see Pastor Hu's smiling face.

"Here is our friend, Mr. Qiu (CHEW) and his son," he announced.

Surprised, Gerhard invited the men into his study. Both the Chinese pastor and Gerhard explained the way of salvation to them. Then Gerhard looked directly at Mr. Qiu.

"Have you given your heart to Jesus? Do you believe that He can save your soul and heal your body?"

"Yes, I did that last night," said the man. "Now I am willing to stay here until I am free from the curse of opium."

Gerhard studied the man's face. Already he looked different. He had taken a bath and changed his ragged clothes. A look of determination was in his eyes.

Gerhard turned to the addict's son, a well-dressed young man.

"I have two things to ask you. First, are you

willing to come to church with your father if he is cured? Then, if the Lord would take your father to his heavenly home, are you willing to pay for the funeral expenses?"

The son stood up. Drawing a deep breath, he said, "Mr. Foreigner, we have a prosperous firecracker business. We are not poor. In fact, my father's splendid coffin sits in our front room. If he dies, it is nothing to us. He's just an opium devil anyway."

Gerhard was taken back by the son's disrespect.

"Remember, he is still your honorable father," Gerhard gently chided the man.

"True," the son replied, bowing his head. "We have never stopped hoping he would change."

Gerhard gave Mr. Qiu a small room in the back of the chapel. Every day Christian workers stayed at his side teaching him God's Word and praying with him. And every day, as his faith grew stronger, his fight against the powers of darkness grew greater.

His suffering increased until he could neither eat nor sleep. The whole compound was disturbed by his horrible cries. It seemed he could not survive. But, as the Christians sang and prayed in Jesus' name, the pain gradually decreased and the demons fled.

On the tenth day, Mr. Qiu lay like a dead man. Mrs. Hu came into the room with a pot of tea and a spoon.

"As soon as he opens his eyes," she told the helper, "we will feed him as much of this tea as he can take. Then gradually he will be able to take food."

Little by little Mr. Qiu's strength returned. A month later, as a happy Christian newly delivered from the opium habit, he left the compound.

"See what Jesus has done for the old opium devil," he declared up and down the streets. His son and the whole Qiu family were converted to Christ.

It was New Years—the Chinese New Year—complete with its idolatrous celebrations. Houses were carefully cleaned to sweep out all the evil. The kitchen god was taken down and honey smeared over his mouth before it was thrown into the fire. The honey assured, they said, that only good things would be reported about the family. Then a new god was pasted on the wall.

All debts from the past year had to be paid unless the debtor fled the country for four months. On both sides and over the top of the door red good luck signs were pasted for the family's blessing. Some even killed a chicken and smeared its blood over the door frames. (Because of these traditions, scholars have wondered if at one time the Chinese knew about the blood atonement of the Old Testament.) Popping firecrackers split the air day and night.

The first day of the New Year was celebrated with feasting and a family get-together. Stores closed for two full days. Gifts of sweets and fruits were exchanged between relatives and friends. The favorite was date-filled mooncakes, delicious beyond description.

All sorts of gambling was permitted. It began simply, but before long gamblers gathered in great numbers behind closed doors. Large amounts were now at stake. Gambling and drinking persisted until some lost all they owned, even to the clothes on their backs.

The young gambler who chopped off his finger called on Gerhard the second day of the new year. Although his finger was still painful, all seemed to be well with the young man. However, a few days later he appeared again looking as if he hadn't slept for several nights. He had gone back to gambling. Not only had the young man's addiction resulted in physical mutilation, it was now evident that it had taken its toll psychologically and spiritually as well.

But a larger crisis loomed in the country—a political one. Armies from the southern capital of Canton were fighting against the armies of the northern capital, Beijing. There were two capitals—Canton and Beijing, and two presidents—Dr. Sun Yat Sen (SOON yat SEN) and Li Yuan-Hung (LEE YOU ahn HOONG) respectively. And a young officer named Chiang Kai-shek was leading his Soviet-trained troops from the northern armies. Province after province had capitulated to them.

At the annual Mission conference, reports surfaced of fierce fighting and terrible famines. Men were reduced to eating women and children while others ate clay from the field. Thousands perished daily. It was at this conference that Howard Van Dyke and Gerhard were assigned to survey the poor, neglected, unevanglized province of South Anhui for possible missionary occupation.

Somewhere in South Anhui there are precious pearls to be found for the Master, Gerhard thought. And then out loud he prayed, "Lord, if I'm assigned to South Anhui, I'm willing to go."

God was about to take him at his word.

10

The Dragon's Fury: Taiping

Sparkling frost crystals spangled field and forest, reflecting like diamonds on the crusty edges of the ruts along the road. Two men in deep conversation were walking as briskly as their heavily quilted garments allowed. This was the first of three days it would be until Gerhard and Pastor Hu arrived at their destination, the city of Taiping.

Ahead, several carriers trotted along with baggage swaying rhythmically from their carrying poles. Trailing between, carrying his bundle over his shoulders, was a peasant in a wide straw hat. He whistled tunelessly between his teeth.

"Hu, I can't believe you did that!" commented Gerhard as he burst into a hearty laugh.

"But, I did, Sen Mushe. What else could I do? When I got your letter I went immediately to Taiping Xian (SHEE en) (Taiping City, a county seat) and found a needy widow who was willing to rent her property. Two witnesses were present when the contract was signed in the name of the Xuan Dau Hui (SHOW en DAW WHAY) (The Christian and Missionary Alliance). How did I know that the woman thought she was renting to a Mr. Xuan instead of to our 'Proclaiming the Doctrine Mission'?" Both men chuckled. "Later, of course, I felt sorry for her. When the townspeople found out what she had done, they confiscated her property and threw her out on the street."

"Is it true that her problems have something to do with the infamous Taiping Rebellion?" Gerhard asked.

"Yes, Pastor," Hu answered. "In 1851 a man named Hung overthrew the Imperial Qings (CHINGS). The rebellion started in Canton where Hung claimed he had a vision of Jesus Christ whom he called his Older Brother. Christ, he said, had directed him to overthrow the corrupt Qing Dynasty and lead China into a new day.

"At first Hung's principles were Christian and his army well disciplined. But as he conquered cities and provinces, things changed. Money and supplies ran low for both armies. They began to inflict brutalities on the people and left great devastation behind. Finally,

Hung captured Nanking and set up his government there. He lived in wealth and gross immorality while continuing to urge his army on to Beijing. They might have destroyed the city and brought an end to the reign of the Manchus had it not been for the aid of the French and British.

"After conquering all eleven provinces, with more than 20 million people losing their lives, the Taiping Rebellion was overthrown. Nanking was sacked and burned. Its leader committed suicide." Pastor Hu paused a moment. "It was a tragic time for my parents who lived in the Yangtze Valley."

"So what has that got to do with the widow who rented a house to our Mission?" inquired Gerhard.

"Well, Hung's followers captured the city and the people fled to the mountains. Then people from north of the river came and occupied the vacant city. When the local people returned, they had to fight to regain their homes. It was then the city fathers decreed that if anyone would allow a foreigner, Chinese or otherwise, to purchase property in their city, that person would be beheaded, his family buried alive and the clan's holdings confiscated."

"Now I can see why we will not be welcomed in Taiping Xian," Gerhard said soberly. "Oh, well, I guess instead of Taiping, 'city of peace,' it should be called 'Taiping, city of trouble' as far as we're concerned." Gerhard laughed. But little did he realize how prophetic his words would be.

"According to the posters pasted on the city walls," Pastor Hu continued, "the magistrate has promised a substantial reward to anyone who will kill us if we return."

There was a slight pause.

"After the past weeks of prayer and fasting I'm sure we can stand on the promises the Lord has given to us," the missionary responded. The two men walked on quietly for a time.

"If we didn't have the assurance that this was the Lord's time for us to enter Taiping Xian, I would never venture to go there," Gerhard said finally, breaking the silence. "With men expecting a reward for our head, the enemy is doing his best to keep us out." The comment brought only a low hum from Pastor Hu.

By late evening the men were at the gates of Qingyang (CHING yahng). Once in the city, the travelers walked through narrow, dimly lit streets filled with the voices of children and the calls of water-sellers. Smoke curled from red joss sticks stuck in the cracks of the cobblestones in front of small idols.

Gerhard led the way to the iron gates of the Mission and called for the gatekeeper. Cries of surprise greeted the party. The gatekeeper brought Gerhard to the Mission house and knocked. Lida White, a tall, fair-skinned, red-haired lady opened it.

"Brother Jacobson, I'm so glad you've come," she said. "This is the most difficult Christmas we've ever had. Fred Page and his wife brought a demon-oppressed woman from the Wuchang Bible Institute. We have her here in our home until she can be delivered." Lida's face was ashen from exhaustion. Dark shadows underlined her blue eyes.

"We have been praying for Mrs. Wang for more than a week and the demon's power is weakening. However, he claims she is his property and he will not leave," she continued. "I hope you will stay and help us pray for her."

Before Gerhard could answer, the door was suddenly pulled open and a wild-eyed woman in disheveled clothes appeared. Strings of hair hung across her face.

Pointing an accusing finger at Gerhard, the woman screamed, "I know who you are. You're Pastor Jacobson." Then, pointing to herself, she continued, "I'm the devil and I'm going to enter you and use you for my purposes."

Fear gripped Gerhard's heart. *Why did I ever stop at Qingyang?* he wondered. Cold sweat broke over him. "Oh God," he whispered, "how can I help in this situation when I'm so fearful myself?"

Instantly Gerhard felt a surge of power, like water flowing through his body and falling like a cool shower from his head to his feet. He looked at the floor. There was no water there.

Instead, an invisible Presence enfolded him in a cloud of peace and love.

"No, you can't do that," Gerhard responded authoritatively, addressing the demon's threat. "I belong to the Lord Jesus and His precious blood covers me."

As the missionaries talked around the supper table that evening, Fred Page told Gerhard the story of Mrs. Wang. She was a Christian who had married an unbeliever. Since there were few women workers in the church she had asked permission to take a short training course at the Wuchang Bible Institute. There, through depression, doubts and fits of anger, her problems had surfaced. In order not to disrupt the school, the Pages had brought her to Qingyang until she could be delivered.

For the next three days Gerhard and the Taiping party stayed to pray for the troubled woman. At last, Mrs. Wang was led to pray, "Lord Jesus, I ask You to deliver me from all the power of Satan."

There was a great difference in her after that prayer. Instead of two personalities with two mannerisms, Mrs. Wang's sweet spirit returned. Gone was the mannish voice, the snarls and hatred, the screams and the fear at the sight and prayers of the Christians. Now she was saying, "*Ping an*. Peace be to you," whenever she met them.

It was New Year's day when Gerhard and his party set out again for the mountains which rose majestically on the horizon. A great white heron spread its silver wings over the dry stubble of the rice fields as it awakened to meet the morning sun. Gracefully it moved up and down, now against the purple mountains, now against the pale blue sky. *God has made everything to praise Him,* Gerhard mused. *Oh, that my heart would feel as free and trusting as the birds.* The miles toward the dreaded city of Taiping shortened with each step.

It was late afternoon when the men entered Taiping. The sun, a great orange ball of fire, sank behind the mountains bathing everything in its crimson glow. Pastor Hu led the way to the building he had rented on one of the narrow streets. Its great iron doors had already been barricaded for the night.

"*Kai men, kai men! Ke ren lai liau.* Open the door, guests have come," the pastor called, careful not to reveal their identity.

"Please come in," said a sweet voice as a girl with golden earrings flashing between thick braids slid the heavy bolt and eased the door open.

It was not just the caretaker's family that had taken up residence in the house, but a number of his relatives as well. While people and things were being shuffled around to make room for the travelers, others from the street were pushing into the courtyard. News of the foreigner's arrival had traveled fast.

Soon more than 400 people filled the place, their expressions angry and menacing.

"Qui, take my card to the *yamen* (office of the magistrate) and have the magistrate send the military protection he promised. Quickly," Gerhard urged the cook. In no time, twenty-four soldiers arrived to take charge.

Gerhard walked in and out among the crowd listening to their conversation.

"Please, Mr. Foreigner," pleaded the captain, grasping Gerhard by the arm, "your life is in danger. Go into the building and stay in one of the back rooms. I'll have a guard at your door."

But Gerhard was not content to be confined to a guarded room. Repeatedly he walked through the crowd trying to catch their mood. And, each time, he was escorted back by the soldiers until the captain said roughly, "Mr. Sen, if this mob becomes violent and you lose your head, I will lose mine also."

Reluctantly Gerhard decided it was time to retire for the night. The men put up Gerhard's camp cot and mosquito net. The cook busily fried fish on the kerosene pressure stove.

"From now on we'll be living like goldfish in a bowl, Pastor Sen," Pastor Hu said with a twinkle in his eye. "Listen to what the people are saying, 'They pump up their light and it shines like the sun. They pump up their stove and it burns the rice. But the foreign devil dresses and eats like we do. That's good.' "

After the evening meal, the men gathered for Bible reading and prayer. "The LORD is my light and my salvation—whom shall I fear? The LORD is the stronghold of my life—of whom shall I be afraid?" (Psalm 27:1) Comforted by God's Word, they went to bed in their clothes. By midnight only about 100 people remained on the compound.

At dawn Gerhard was awakened by a clatter of buckets and the chatter of women. A strong toilet stench pervaded the air.

"Pastor Sen, come quickly," Pastor Hu called. "There are many women here who are going to pour night soil all over the place."

"We've got to stop them," Gerhard called back, rushing out just in time to see several dozen women with their buckets in the air ready to dump. Ordinarly these women took human manure in thirty-gallon clay jars from the city's latrines to the vegetable gardens outside the city.

"We're going to stink you out of here," a lanky, red-faced woman threatened, swinging her jars ominously from her carrying poles.

"If you dump that stuff, either you or we will have something unfortunate happen to us before evening," Gerhard retorted. But the women didn't budge. In fact, they stayed all day threatening to carry out their plans. Gerhard and the pastor tried to reason with them, but to no avail. Gradually, as the sun began to set, the women drifted away, promising to return the next day.

11

The Dragon's Fury: The Ultimatum

One frosty morning in January a young man arrived at Gerhard's residence. His clothes were an ill-fitting gray. His eyes shifted from side to side and around the room. His hand gripped a wrinkled paper.

"It's for the foreigner," the young man muttered, thrusting the paper toward Pastor Hu.

"What is it about?" Gerhard asked nonchalantly as he turned down the pressure stove.

"It is a bill for some opium you purchased recently."

Gerhard felt the blood rise in his throat. He wanted to blast the young man and throw him out. *Who does he think I am? Doesn't he realize I know it's a crime to deal in opium? Lock him in a room in the back until we can send a letter to the magistrate*. Instead, Gerhard asked the man to sit down while Pastor Hu got out his brushes, rice paper and block of ink. A letter, expressing his feelings more accurately, was soon on its way to the *yamen*.

Within a few hours, a response from the magistrate arrived. It read: "Although the law demands the death penalty for anyone dealing with opium, we are honoring your request that this young man be beaten and detained in jail." What actually transpired, Gerhard did not know, but one thing he was certain of: he had evidently escaped another attack of Satan on his ministry in Taiping.

But more were on the way.

February drew to a close. The gray skies threatened snow. Cook Qiu had just come back from the market deeply dejected. No one in town or at the market would sell him any food.

"Listen, brother," Gerhard declared, "the Lord hasn't forsaken us yet. Remember our verse this morning? 'Are not five sparrows sold for two pennies? . . . You are worth more than many sparrows' (Luke 12:6-7). Here take this money and go to the farmers. They'll sell."

At noon Qiu returned loaded with cabbages, eggs, chickens, rice and other produce. And at the back gate, stacks of wood were piled high.

"The farmer said he would bring as much as we need when these run out," Qiu reported.

Several other tests awaited the men.

Early one morning as Qiu went to the well to fill his water buckets, an elderly woman in the shadows of her doorway beckoned to him.

"Don't go to the well," she warned. "It was poisoned last night."

Qiu hurried back to the house, his empty buckets clunking along beside him.

"Now we'll die," he moaned.

Gerhard slapped his knee and laughed.

"They can't outdo us! The river is frozen over. Break up some ice and bring it home," he replied, giving Qiu a playful shove out the door.

"What are they going to do with that, cook it or fry it?" the street people sneered.

"We don't drink well water anymore," Qiu answered. "The foreigner prefers river water." The day ended with Gerhard making ice cream with evaporated milk—a special dessert.

That night, about midnight, Pastor Hu and Gerhard were awakened by a heavy pounding in the reception hall.

"What on earth is going on, Pastor Hu?" Gerhard shouted as he jumped out of bed. The two men walked into the hall. Several carpenters were hanging a large sign high on the wall. In gold letters it read, "Ancestral Hall."

"Don't be surprised if we get a summons from the *yamen*, Sen Mushe," the pastor remarked wisely. "They'll tell us what this is all about."

Sure enough, the next morning a guard handed the pastor the expected notice. Gerhard and Pastor Hu were to appear at the *yamen.* So, with guards in front and others behind, the two sedan chairs were carried through the *yamen* gates. The magistrate dispensed with the usual formalities and came quickly to the point.

"You noticed, didn't you, gentlemen, that the reception room in your building now has the sign 'Ancestral Hall'?" he asked abruptly.

The pastors acknowledged his remarks with assents and bows.

"Well, Mr. Sen, we regard our ancestral halls as you do your churches and so we are requesting that you vacate the place so we can retain it as such."

Hu nudged Gerhard.

"Ask him why the former family had no ancestral tablets there," he whispered.

With much throat-clearing and bows, Gerhard asked the question.

"That is beside the point," the magistrate answered stiffly. With that, he and his guards got up and left the room. Once again the enemy had been foiled. Gerhard and Pastor Hu left the *yamen* praising the Lord.

The sun was shining in all its brilliance on the newly fallen snow when a runner from the *yamen* rushed in. In his hand was another summons for Gerhard and Pastor Hu to appear before the town officials immediately.

A crease spread across the missionary's forehead as he read it. There was something unusually ominous in the wording of this summons. Pastor Hu and Gerhard decided to spend some time in special prayer before responding. What Gerhard could not know or foresee at that moment was that the next three days would be ones he would never forget. He later recorded the events in his diary:

> As we stood before this powerful Chinese official, I felt the awesome powers of darkness surrounding me. There were stern-looking bodyguards in full regalia. The magistrate himself wore a vivid red, silk jacket. His high mandarin hat had a dangling golden tassel. His manner was icy. After the usual formalities, he cleared his throat importantly.
> "Mr. Sen, do you believe in honoring the powers that be?" he asked haughtily.
> "I most certainly do, Mr. Magistrate," I said bowing politely.
> He seemed pleased and grunted approvingly.
> "If you do, you will obey me when I request that you and your men leave Taiping Xian as soon as possible. If you do as I command," the magistrate continued, "I will invite all the important people of the county to our county-seat for a feast. We will send you away as an outgoing official with an honor guard, firecrackers and a parade. If you refuse, I will take away your protection. You will be left alone. The men hired and paid to kill you will kill you." The face of the official was black with rage, his voice harsh.
> "Thank you, sir," Gerhard responded meekly. "I have appreciated your kindness and the soldiers protecting us. But after the letters from the governor of the province and the American consul in

Shanghai advising you to protect my life, I don't believe that you will withdraw your men."

"I will! You will see by tomorrow," the magistrate shouted as he stalked out arrogantly, a deep scowl creasing his face. The bodyguards saluted and marched out behind him.

The next morning when Gerhard awoke, the soldiers had left. Once more Pastor Hu sat down to write a letter to the magistrate: "Dear sir," Gerhard dictated, "God is my protector. I am ready to live or die for Him. We have decided to remain in the city...."

What followed were three days and nights of terror. Gerhard wrote Alma:

> As long as I live I will never forget those three days. The soldiers had left and I was at the mercy of the mob. From a distance I could hear them coming closer, shouting, "*Sha, sha, sha* (Kill, kill, kill)." All hell seemed to break loose.
>
> The big double doors of the main entrance and all other entrances were open day and night. People walked in and out continually. I slept very little. I sat on a narrow wooden bench with my back to the wall. A cold wind was blowing through the house so I had to wear my fur-lined gown and hat. I don't remember eating, but I must have eaten. Hu and I would change places from time to time so that each could rest, read our Bibles and pray.
>
> One thing I will never forget. Although fear and apprehension gripped me, my inner spirit felt calm and even bold at times. Promises kept flooding my mind, verses I had learned in Bible school: "Thus far has the Lord helped us;" "I will trust and not be afraid" (Isaiah 12:2) and many more.

> Sometimes I became tired of sitting and was curious to hear what the crowd was whispering, so I went and walked among them. I heard them urge each other: "You've got a big knife under your gown, rush him. I'll back you up." Miraculously no one moved. I was greatly strengthened by Psalm 62, "Trust in him at all times . . . pour out your hearts to him, for God is our refuge." I felt your prayers, dearest, and the prayers of friends back home.

After three days, Gerhard decided to do something about the situation. He would escape out the back door at night and travel to the nearest city where he could find a telegraph station and wire for another missionary to come to their aid.

That evening, with a biting wind whirling snow around him, Gerhard crept into the night.

12

The Dragon Is Defeated: "Fear Not"

The city was dark and silent by early dawn. The gamblers had gone to bed. Only the morning star, blinking between scurrying clouds, shone fitfully. Gerhard crept through the narrow eastern gate of Taiping, his chair bearers with him. From the north a gray cloud was advancing rapidly. A tumult of whirling snow soon forced him into the comfort of the sedan chair. He hugged his *hungr* (charcoal burner) for warmth and comfort.

That evening, with only brief stops for tea and to refill the *hungr*, the men reached Shih Tai (SHI TIE). Feeling sick from the cold and exhaustion, Gerhard crawled up into the loft at the inn and flopped down on the straw. *How good it feels to stretch out,* he thought as his mind receded into fitful sleep.

"Sen Mushe! Sen Mushe!"

Was it a dream? Gerhard turned over in the straw. Again, "Sen Mushe! Sen Mushe!" now loud and urgent. Gerhard opened the small wooden shutter and looked out. But even with the light of his newly acquired flashlight he could see no one. He stumbled down the ladder.

A young soldier handed him a card. It was from Mr. Carter, his missionary colleague who lived at Wanchir (WAHN jer), a five-day journey from Taiping. On the card were the words, "Return at once."

What does "return at once" mean? To where? When? Should I start out now or wait until dawn? And what could have prompted Mr. Carter to travel five days to Taiping? It must have been important. Gerhard decided to start out immediately.

"Can you carry me back to Taiping at once?" he asked the sleepy chairbearers.

"How much will you pay us if we do?" the head man inquired.

"I'll pay you double fare."

"We can't start out on empty stomachs. It's a long way in this bad weather, you know."

"I'll see what I can do," Gerhard promised, not knowing if a meal at this time of the night was even a possibility. But the innkeeper complied, and soon the men were slurping bowls of hot rice and vegetables.

Outside, the sky was now clear, the stars brilliant, the road slippery. Leaving the town behind and approaching the river, the men called for the ferry to take them across. A mumbled response echoed from inside the straw hut.

"He says that his boat is anchored out in the river for fear of bandits. It is the only safe place for it. He says we should look for a bridge down river."

The bridge, such as it was, turned out to be several bamboo poles lashed together over a racing mountain stream. Ice and snow had glazed it so that the men had to cross on hands and knees even as it swayed precariously under their weight.

Now a bitter wind was whirling around the dark figures. Above, clouds blotted out the starlight. On the ground, snow obliterated the path. Where was the main road?

"Where are you? Where are we?" the men called frantically as they searched.

"The road to Taiping is over here," someone to the left shouted. But "over here" turned out to be a rice field.

"No, it's over there!" "Over there" led to a grove of bamboos.

"I see a light," another said. The others joined and everyone stumbled toward it. The men ran their hands along the side of the building, feeling for the door.

"Can you tell us how we can get to the road to Taiping?" they called out to whomever might be inside. There was no response. Instead, the tiny light in the window was extinguished.

"They think we are robbers and are afraid to open up," one carrier told the men.

The next harrowing hours were spent roaming in the darkness. At one point they came upon another hut—or was it the same one? Once again, no one would answer their cries for fear of robbers.

At last, as the first light of dawn broke, they found the elusive road and also an inn.

"Listen, men," Gerhard explained, as the chair bearers squatted on the ground drinking tea. "I have to get to Taiping as soon as possible. What will you charge to run the rest of the way?"

"Are you willing to pay us double again?" their leader asked, squinting into Gerhard's blue eyes. "It's four hours from here."

"Agreed," muttered Gerhard.

It was nearly noon when the weary party arrived at the Mission gate. There stood a smiling Mr. Carter.

"Hurry up," he said abruptly, "the magistrate will soon be here."

"Have you called on him already?" Gerhard inquired.

"Yes, and he's returning the favor. I've a long story to tell you. Get going, Brother Jake!"

Gerhard was happy to be able to shave and change from his wet and muddy clothes. Pastor Hu hovered over him like a mother hen.

"I'm so glad you're here," Pastor Hu told him. "They nearly drove me out of the city, but Pastor Carter rescued me. Praise the Lord!"

There was a shout at the gate as the magistrate's chair arrived. The men ushered him and his entourage in with the usual formalities. Surprise registered on the magistrate's face when he saw Gerhard.

"How is it you're here?" he asked brusquely. "I heard you'd left the city. Did you or didn't you?"

Gerhard responded evasively.

"It beats all how you foreigners can travel," the magistrate sputtered.

After everyone was seated around a table of sweetmeats and tea, the magistrate cleared his throat officiously.

"Mr. Sen, you have a fine friend here." Mr. Carter acknowledged the compliment. "He has requested sixty soldiers for your protection and I'm sending them tomorrow." The magistrate smiled magnanimously.

Gerhard rose and bowed deeply.

"How kind of you!" he said.

"But I have a proposition to make to you foreigners. The city officials have decided that there can be an exchange of properties. We have several to offer. Would you care to look at them?"

So that's why I was called back, Gerhard thought. *Now it all makes sense.*

With a mutual commitment to meet again,

the magistrate, obviously pleased with himself, flounced out the door.

Qiu quickly went about preparing the usual meal of rice and cabbage with a few slivers of pork. Gerhard was eager to hear what had prompted Francis Carter to make the five-day trip from Wanchir to Taiping.

"What made you come all this way, Carter?" Gerhard asked. "It must have been very important."

Mr. Carter swallowed another bite.

"Well, on Sunday, after the services and our noon meal, I told my wife, 'Edith, I'm worried about Brother Jacobson there in Taiping. I feel impressed by the Lord to leave immediately to go and see him.' She helped me pack and I left as soon as I could. I arrived none too soon—the mob was ready to throw Pastor Hu out of the city."

"How did you know where our place was?" Gerhard asked, stifling a yawn brought on by the warmth of the room and the hot meal.

"I didn't betray the fact that I was a missionary to those at the inn. I asked them if there were any foreigners in the city. The old innkeeper told me they didn't want any foreigners here. They had refused the Standard Oil people, the Singer Sewing Machine Company and others. But he did say that there was a young American here trying to start a Mission. He had his wife lead me to your place. That's how I got here."

"How did you get along with the magistrate and his men?" Gerhard asked looking quizzically at Mr. Carter.

"He's a wily fellow," Carter responded with a knowing look. "He boasted that, during the Boxer Rebellion in 1900, twenty-six Alliance missionaries were beheaded in his county alone. I didn't act impressed. Instead, I reminded him that I knew he had just received a telegram from the American consul in Shanghai requesting protection for us. He countered by saying that he also knew you had received a telegram advising that we were to settle things with him and the city officials as soon as possible."

"What do you think we should do, Carter?" Gerhard asked, a deep frown wrinkling his forehead.

"Let's first get an appeal for the widow, our landlady. She is now living on the street and her middleman, who made the deal for this place with us, is in jail. Then we can look at the proposed properties later."

"Fine idea, Carter. But right now, I think we'd better rest and have a time of prayer. Then we'll plan together."

When the men awoke the next morning, they were surprised to find that another missionary had come from over the eastern hills. It was tall, lanky William Shantz, one of their senior missionaries, lovingly called "Daddy" or "Bishop" Shantz. According to Pastor Hu, he too was tired and had climbed the ladder to the loft for a sleep.

The aroma of frying fish urged Gerhard off the bed. *Qiu is trying to impress our visitors with his cooking,* Gerhard smiled to himself. Nearby, another ladder squeaked as Mr. Shantz descended slowly into the room.

"Did you have a comfortable rest?" Gerhard asked the bishop after they had exchanged greetings.

"I don't know, Brother." Mr. Shantz's voice was soft and high. "I seemed to have had a dream that a snake was crawling over me. Or maybe it wasn't a dream."

Gerhard shrugged his shoulders and winked at Mr. Carter who had joined them.

"Don't be afraid, Daddy. It might be my house snake. He's good at keeping the rats from the straw mattresses up there."

"I think I'll sleep downstairs tonight." Mr. Shantz grimaced and laughed. He selected one of the side rooms and Pastor Hu pasted oil paper over the holes in the window squares to keep out the cold wind and peeping eyes.

That evening when all were in bed, there was a knock at the gate. Pastor Hu let the man in even though he was suspicious of his intentions.

"May I talk to you in your inner room?" the stranger asked Gerhard.

"Only if you let me bring the pastor along," the missionary replied cautiously.

"Don't be afraid, Sen Mushe. I'm your friend," the man smiled. "I'm not here to harm you."

"I think he's an honest man, Sen Mushe," Pastor Hu advised, urging Gerhard to go with the man.

After the two were seated, he began.

"You recall the three days and nights when your life was in danger?"

Gerhard nodded. It was all too recently etched into his memory.

"I knew the mob was determined to kill you," the man continued, his face pale, his voice trembling. "You see, I'm not a local man. I come from north of the river. Those nights when you were in danger, I called my friends to come and help you." His words caught in his throat as he glanced furtively at the door. "During those nights I had 200 men armed with sticks, knives and a few guns ready to protect you in case the mob attacked."

"I'm deeply touched and thank you from my heart," Gerhard replied. "I'm sure it was God who raised up you and your friends to help me. Are you a Christian?"

"No, Pastor Sen, but I have met some travelers who were selling books that tell about Jesus Christ. See, I have one here." He pulled a Gospel portion from his pocket. Gerhard knew the man had encountered one of the colporteurs.

The stranger left with a warning.

THE DRAGON IS DEFEATED: "FEAR NOT"

"Don't mention my visit to anyone or I'll lose my head," he said faintly as Pastor Hu led him out through the back gate of the compound.

During the next few days the missionaries went to plead the case of the widow and her middleman. They managed to secure the middleman's release and the widow was allowed to stay with her relatives. The next task was to visit the properties so highly recommended by the magistrate.

Several days were spent looking over buildings and parcels of land unsuitable for the Mission—a ploy by the magistrate to discourage the missionaries.

The first was a vacant lot in a field surrounded by graves. It was totally unsuitable. Next they went to a ruined temple.

"Now this is an ideal place," the middleman bragged.

"We especially like this wide frontage," Mr. Shantz commented.

"Hmm, I'm sorry, but the frontage is not included," the middleman coughed apologetically. *Just how then would one get to the place?* Gerhard wondered. He decided not to ask the obvious.

Mr. Carter and Daddy Shantz had to leave. Now, once again, Gerhard was alone. Thankfully, the presence of the sixty guards brought a certain calm to the situation. The street people lost interest. Farmers were busy preparing fields and gardens for planting. Only when something unexpected took place did the mob congregate. It was about to happen!

Spring was finally here. The icy grip of winter had indeed been broken. A soft south wind blew the fragrant smell of wild flowers from the hill behind the house into the bedroom where Gerhard lay suffering from a sticky rash. Despite the discomfort of the rash—and the beautiful spring air—Gerhard's mind was elsewhere, a kind of darkness settling over him.

He recalled how bravely he and Pastor Hu had set out from Datong to come to Taiping. He could still see their families waving and smiling tearfully as the men started down the road. Now Gerhard knew he was jeopardizing his family's future. If the murderous mob had its way, there was no doubt that his children would be left fatherless.

In his mind he saw Alma, Mother Sarah and his little daughters—Doris and Winifred—in a frenzy of weeping around his casket. A heart-rending groan rose from the depths of his being.

That had been three months earlier. Now another fear stalked across his imagination. It was the fear his mother had often spoken of.

"If something happens to you in China, I'll never be able to bear it," she had said. The words reverberated in Gerhard's head: *never be able to bear it; never be able to bear it.*

Then, an even more fearful picture exploded across his mind. It was of his mother prostrate on the floor and his sister Anna frantically trying to revive her. *I must give up my plan for Taiping*, he reasoned.

"Oh, God," he groaned aloud, "help me find a way to escape from this city. I must go quickly."

Then still another wave of fear, like a living thing, threatened to embrace the slender figure in its icy grip.

Suddenly he prayed, "Oh, God, in Jesus' name, I rebuke this spirit of fear." The words came with force and urgency. Almost in reflex action, but still shaking, Gerhard reached for the familiar feel of his leather Bible.

"Be not afraid, neither be thou dismayed," he read, his eyes straining to read the words where the Bible had fallen open, "For the Lord thy God is with thee whithersoever thou goest" (Joshua 1:9, KJV).

Soon the shaking stopped as the words of challenge and promise reached their comforting fingers deep into Gerhard's soul.

13

The Dragon Is Defeated: A New Attitude, a New Church

"**P**astor Jacobson, Pastor Jacobson!" Pastor Hu, his long gown flapping, shouted at the top of his voice, interrupting Gerhard's reverie. "Another big crowd is coming. Can't you hear the noise?"

Another crowd! *With so many these last few months, what could another be?* wondered Gerhard. Rising slowly from his cot, he laid his Bible aside and pushed back a shock of dark hair from his forehead. Groping for a small bamboo chair, he carefully raised himself to the high window.

"There are two sedan chairs and some carriers with baggage coming this way," continued Pastor Hu, balancing on a stool of his own.

"Whoever it is, it's not the magistrate's official chair or any other chair from the *yamen*," Gerhard muttered aloud.

The shouting grew louder as the little parade advanced down the dusty road. Soon it was evident that the crowd was mostly women and children. *Ah, no need to fear this parade,* Gerhard thought as he allowed his muscles to relax.

"Oh, no! Impossible! It's Alma, Doris and the Bible woman!"

Gerhard jumped down from the stool and ran to open the front door.

The curtains of the sedan chair pushed back as Mrs. Li, the Bible woman, helped a small, young woman and little girl to the street. The chair bearers were shouting, driving the crowds away with spicy curses that left embarrassed looks on the sea of dark faces.

Gerhard was about to pull his wife into his embrace when he remembered Chinese etiquette. It was considered improper to show affection between the sexes in public. So he picked up little Doris and gave her a tight hug.

Pastor Hu was already dickering with the carriers. Mrs. Li was shouting to the men and directing traffic toward the large reception room where the bags were to be placed. The street seemed enveloped in utter confusion.

"I told you not to come to Taiping," Gerhard

shouted above the din. "It's very dangerous here, Alma. Why did you come?"

"The Lord told me to come," his petite wife answered self-assuredly as she struggled to lift a box into the room.

Gerhard bent over the boxes.

"It's good to see you, darling," he said somewhat more gently, "but it makes the situation worse than ever with you two here."

Out of the corner of his eye Gerhard could see the stout Bible woman hobbling on her bound feet, heading for the kitchen where she would, no doubt, command the crew to make tea for the weary travelers.

Suddenly it seemed that all the weariness Gerhard had accumulated over the last three months drained from his body. It was as if his prison-house existence was gone forever. He rushed to the cupboard where his few household utensils were stored and began setting a square wooden table.

Looking at his wife, he paused.

"Well, you always do what you want, Alma," he said with a slight smile. "Anyway, I'm thanking the Lord you arrived today since you did decide to come."

"Why is that, Gay?" Alma asked using the abbreviation she reserved for intimate discussions with her husband. Then, without waiting for a reply, she continued, "This is a nice big room for services, but it's so dark and stuffy. Can't we open the doors a bit?"

"And have everyone cramming in to stare at us?"

"Oh yes, of course. We all had to have our skin and hair felt every time people got near enough to touch us as we came into the city. They thought Doris's brown hair was golden."

Alma glanced at the diminutive five-year-old running from corner to corner, delightedly squealing something in Chinese at each new discovery. Her little yellow, pongee silk dress fluttered like butterfly wings in the dark shadows.

"So why did you feel my coming to Taiping today was so providential?" Alma asked again, this time waiting for a reply.

"Actually, my faith was at its lowest point since coming here," Gerhard replied quietly. "I was just sitting on the cot in the next room thinking about how to get out, and . . ."

"You'd never leave after this long a time," Alma interjected. "You're not a stubborn Swede for nothing." Her girlish laugh brought stares from the Chinese in the room.

Alma's coming did much to improve the tiresome diet that Gerhard and Pastor Hu had become accustomed to. *It's good to have my wife by my side,* Gerhard mused. But the itch persisted, stubbornly refusing to respond to any treatment.

"If the Lord doesn't do something for me, I'm leaving this place, honey. I can't take it much longer."

It's not like Gerhard to give up. Obviously the emotional, physical and spiritual strain are taking their toll, Alma thought as she put her arm around Gerhard's shoulders and squeezed.

"This rash is another attack of the enemy on you," Alma said authoritatively. "Let's spend time in prayer and claim your deliverance." Alma and Gerhard bowed their heads, earnestly asking God for a breakthrough in the situation.

In the middle of the prayer, Gerhard shouted, "Alma, I don't feel anything. The itch has stopped."

The next day Gerhard's skin was clear, the rash totally gone. And with it, the heaviness that had been about to crush his spirit.

Little Doris was getting restless without her sisters and her toys.

"Mama, can we go for a walk?" she pleaded one day.

"Yes. Get your hat on. We'll call your daddy."

Gerhard was dumbfounded at the idea.

"Alma, I can't go out, even by the back gate, and neither can you!" he told his wife. "We're prisoners here."

"Oh, foolishness!" Alma said, cocking her head to one side. "Come on, let's go." Pastor Hu agreed with Alma. A walk would do them all good.

It was thrilling to be out again. Spring was in the air. The peach trees were budding. Birds

THE DRAGON IS DEFEATED: A NEW ATTITUDE

were calling to each other. The villagers were delighted to see Alma and especially Doris. Each time they stopped to feel her soft white skin and hair, Doris squirmed.

"Why do they always have to touch me, Mother?" she complained.

"Be patient, dearest. They just want to make friends," Alma assured her little daughter.

From that day on, Alma, Gerhard and Doris took a daily afternoon stroll and slowly the people of Taiping changed their attitude toward the Mission.

A short three weeks later, Alma and Doris returned to Datong. They all knew it would be hard for Gerhard to be alone again, but the change of attitude on the part of the city was cause for great rejoicing. No doubt better days were ahead.

Thunder and lightning broke across the sky as Gerhard walked to the back of the courtyard, the "heavenly well" as they called it. Outside, wind and rain wERE sweeping through the trees and bowing the grass in its path.

From the front door came a loud, insistent pounding.

"Open the gate. Hurry, I'm getting wet!"

"Coming, coming," said the gatekeeper struggling to open his oil paper umbrella. Fighting to keep the gate from hurling him backward, he hung on to it until a drenched Daddy Shantz was safely inside.

"Are you here to see the rest of the properties with me tomorrow?" Gerhard asked, taking the bishop's wet clothes from him.

"Yes, and I hope we can settle on something, don't you?" Daddy Shantz always seemed to appear at just the right time.

The earth had a well-laundered look the next day. Everything sparkled and the sky was cloudless as the missionaries followed the middleman down one narrow street after another, carefully hopping over puddle after puddle.

At a corner, they turned sharply to another busy street where hawkers were advertising their wares and women with babies strapped to their backs hobbled from store to store comparing prices. Quite unexpectedly, four men belonging to the gentry approached them.

"The magistrate asked us to accompany you to see this last piece of property," the tallest one said, bowing courteously.

"Please join us," Mr. Shantz replied, concealing a smile with his hand. "We would appreciate your opinion, I'm sure."

"Oh, here's the place!"

The middleman stopped abruptly in front of a dilapidated building, grAy with age. The former wine factory and shop was set back from the street behind iron gates which hung awkwardly on their hinges. The courtyard was covered with uneven stone pavement. Weeds emerged from every crack.

"Where is the owner?" Mr. Shantz asked the middleman as the party wandered through the reception room and into the side rooms. Windows and doors were missing, rats scurried about and cobwebs hung like sooty black curtains.

"Here is the owner, Mr. Ma," responded the middleman. From nowhere appeared a little old man with a mustache that drooped on both sides of his mouth. He looked up cautiously.

"Are you willing to sell this place, Mr. Ma?" Mr. Shantz asked directly, noting a pervasive apprehension in the man's deeply wrinkled eyes.

"Oh, yes. As you can see, it is of no use to me anymore since I'm old and my sons aren't interested in the business."

"He lost the place through gambling," the middleman whispered into Gerhard's ear.

"According to Chinese custom, I believe the owner is responsible to make improvements before selling. Isn't that right?" The tall man from the gentry stepped forward to reply to Bishop Shantz' question.

"Yes, Mr. Foreigner, that's right. But Mr. Ma is not able to do that. How would it be if Mr. Ma gives you the property at a reduced rate and you make the improvements?"

As the men continued their tour it soon became clear that, despite the state of disrepair of the compound, they had at last found something with potential. It might even be possible that some of the materials from the old wine shop would be usable for a new building. *After all the months of prayer and struggle, could it be that the Mission was actually going to have a place to preach the gospel?* Gerhard wondered almost aloud. It seemed that prayer was being answered right before their eyes, right at that very moment. It was almost too good to be true!

The men sat down beside a rickety, dust-covered table to talk. Three hours later, a tentative price had been reached.

"I'll tell you what we will do," Mr. Shantz said deliberately. "We would like to invite all of you with the magistrate and the city officials for a feast at our place sometime next week. Then final arrangements can be made and we'll sign the documents."

"*Hau, haU,* (HOW, HOW), good, good," everyone responded in unison. After much bowing at the gate and in the street the men parted, smiles creasing every face.

"I'd like to throw my hat in the air and shout 'Praise the Lord!' as loud as I can," Gerhard said, his voice jubilant.

"Wait until we get in the house, Jake!" Mr. Shantz pleaded with a grin.

"Let's stop at the telegraph office on the way home. I need to send three telegrams right away. One to the American consul, another to our Wuchang headquarters and one to Alma. Wouldn't it be great if she and the Bible woman could be here for the official paper signing?"

Mr. Shantz agreed. En route home they also stopped at the cake shop to treat themselves in celebration of the day's discovery.

The events at the Mission house became the talk of the town. The Mission had won their case and were about to obtain property because of Bishop Shantz, the wise old man from Wanchir.

"They've removed all the guards and now the foreigners are protected by law," the people whispered.

The magistrate and his men came to the Mission compound in full military dress. At the feast the missionaries sat next to him in the places of highest honor. After a series of flowery speeches, well wishes for the success of the Mission and praises for the "cooperation" of the city officials, the "red paper" was drawn up. It gave the Mission a 100-year lease on the property. All parties signed. Old Mr. Ma, dressed in his newly acquired silks, beamed and bowed repeatedly.

"We will hold our first public meeting there this Sunday," Gerhard announced before the end of the feast. "Please tell all your friends to come. We want you to hear the good news from God's Word."

The invitation spread like wild fire. Sunday found people from both the city and the countryside crowding into the compound. Those who couldn't get into the building filled the windows and doors. Pastor Hu, the men missionaries and Alma spoke.

An elderly merchant and his family remained behind when the service was dismissed. He bowed deeply several times before he spoke.

"Pastors," he said finally, emotion filling his voice, "we are Christians, the only Christians in Taiping. I want you to know that I have been praying for fifteen years that someone would come to Taiping and preach the gospel. Now I am ready to die." The old man turned his face heavenward. Tears of joy rolled down his wrinkled cheeks. "You have answered my prayer," he concluded. He bowed and shuffled out the door.

Fifteen years! The battle in the heavenlies had been going on for fifteen years. No wonder the opposition had been so fierce. No wonder Gerhard's own heart had at times felt like a battlefield. But during all those years, there had been people of the Pearl in Taiping.

"The dragon is defeated," Gerhard laughed as he picked up a song sheet and moved a chair. "From now on it will be smooth sailing."

"I wouldn't be so sure," responded Daddy Shantz. "The worst may be ahead. Pray on!"

Alma, Gerhard and baby Doris en route to China 1918.

The Datong Mission house where the Jacobsons were stationed 1921-25.

Pastor Hu and his family at Datong. Pastor Hu served as co-pastor with Gerhard and helped to open the work in Taiping.

The Alliance guest house and business department, Hankow, China, 1920s-30s.

Gerhard and his party crawled over this ice-covered bridge in the middle of the night after escaping from Taiping.

Grandma Sarah Amstutz with Doris and Winnie, at Datong, 1921. Grandma arrived in October 1919 to help take care of the children.

The four Jacobson girls, taken in Datong, 1925:
L to R: Bette, Evelyn, Doris and Winnie.

Gerhard with Datong circuit workers, including pastors and the Bible woman, Mrs. Li, second from right.

This converted opium addict from Datong owned a prosperous firecracker business.

The Central China Alliance Mission conference, 1921, the year the Jacobsons joined the Alliance.

The Jacobsons spent an extended furlough at 3045 Clifton Ave. in Chicago.

The Qimen magistrate, second from left,
after a leopard hunt in the Yellow Mountains.

Spending the summer of 1933 at Kuling. L to R back row: Gerhard, Winnie, Doris, Alma; L to R front row: Evelyn, Bette.

Coolies carrying a sedan chair and luggage up the mountain to Jigongshan.

The Jacobson's newly renovated and enlarged home at Jigong, 1937.

Buildings in the foreground are the American School as it was located at Kuling during the time the school was forced to relocate from Jigong, 1930-34.

The American School buildings at Jigong. The building on the right burned during the Japanese war, but was rebuilt under the communists.

A 1982 view of Jigong Mountain.

Gerhard fills his Ford V8 at a Shanghai gas station (1937) before the city was bombed.

The congregation of the North Szechuan Road Alliance Church in Shanghai, 1938. The church was later bombed by the Japanese.

The North Szechuan Road Church showing tower destoyed by bombs.

One of the many holes in the roof of the North Szechuan Road property.

Gerhard, Alma and Matthew Birrel, left, and already baptized Jews, right, flank 32 of the 79 Jewish baptismal candidates in Shanghai.

A view of the Alliance primary and secondary school in Shanghai, later bombed by the Japanese.

A Shanghai Sikh policeman like the one who donated $500 to Gerhard's radio ministry.

Dr. A.C. Snead at a conference at the Szechuan Road church, about 1938; Rev. Arthur Hanson, board representative to the right.

Hundreds pack the auditorium on the top floor of the Sun Company building to hear the gospel preached by Timothy Dzao after the city was bombed.

The four Jacobson sisters attended Nyack College while their father was interned in Shanghai. L to R: Doris, who became a missionary to the Philippines, Winnie, a missionary to China and the Philippines; Bette and Evelyn married and remained in America.

Gerhard and Alma, center, celebrate their golden wedding anniversary, August 18, 1966. Winnie and Doris are to the right of Alma.

The last picture of the Jacobsons together; taken in St. Petersburg, Florida, Easter 1967.

14

Pearls in the Dragon's Lair: Datong

Alma awoke at daybreak. A steady rain was falling. Wind whipped the branches of the rugged pine causing it to scrape noisily against the tin roof of the Shantz house on Jigong Mountain. Fog wrapped the mountain top and distant peaks, their gray-whiteness encompassing the entire region.

Downstairs sounds of breakfast-making could be heard. The tantalizing smell of pancakes and bacon drifted up to the bedroom. Checking to be sure that little Bette was still asleep, Alma dressed and crept softly down the stairs. Mother Sarah was already sitting in a wicker chair near a window, her Bible in her lap, her face gray and fatigued.

"You've had another bad night, Mother?" Alma's voice was gentle.

"Yes. You've been hearing me talk about going to the States, but now I feel the Lord wants me to trust Him to heal my gallstones."

"But the doctor in Hankow suggested an operation. Aren't you going to follow his advice?" Alma seated herself across from her mother and gripped her hand. "We can afford it, I'm sure."

"At the missionary conference there is always a healing service," Sarah continued. "I want the Mission leaders to anoint me and pray for me." Her eyes glanced hopefully at her daughter.

"I'll stand with you, Mother. I know the Lord can work a miracle as we trust Him. I hear the children bouncing around upstairs. I'll get them dressed and we can eat."

Missionaries were arriving daily for the conference. But travel was risky from the cities along the river due to the ongoing war for the unification of China. Bandits often took advantage of the unstable conditions and pillaged the river vessels. One report during the conference recounted a terrifying attack made on a launch on which eighteen missionaries were traveling. Bandits on the shore fired on the ship killing many passengers. But all the missionaries escaped harm.

The conference messages, especially the one on "The Lord Our Healer," were deeply moving. As planned, Sarah was prayed for and, although she felt no immediate change, time would reveal that she was completely delivered from any further gallstone trouble.

After one of the sessions, Mrs. Birrel, the chairman's wife, took Alma and Gerhard aside.

"The committee has asked me to talk to you about your next assignment before it is read from the floor. You are free to let us know first if you agree to it. You are assigned to Datong."

Mrs. Birrel paused to let the words sink in.

"Taiping is far inland," she continued, "and not suitable for the children, as your quarters are on the second floor of the new building and there is no yard. Besides, supplies and medical aid in an emergency are five days' journey away. At Datong," she continued, "the doctor at Wuhu can easily be reached."

Tall, genteel Mrs. Birrel looked anxiously at Alma. She felt her face turn red. *Do they suspect my morning stomach upsets are because I'm pregnant again? I hope not,* she thought.

"We will pray about the assignment," Gerhard said finally. "Thank you for letting us know in advance." He stood to his feet and shook hands with the chairman's wife.

That night the wind moaned outside the house. Rain pelted the roof. Lightning flashed in the windows. Gerhard slept little. A deep agony filled his soul as he recalled the previous summer when he had made his commitment to the Lord to go to Taiping. It had been a difficult decision. He had pondered it long. Yes, it was true—the place was not easily accessible, the food was poor, the dialect different. Dangers from bandits were real. *Hardly a place for a family,* Gerhard decided.

He remembered how one night, as he was about to fall asleep, he had had a dream. Or was it a vision? Gently, so as not to awaken Alma, he slipped out of bed to find the account in his diary.

He began to read.

> I had a strange and wonderful dream last night. On the bed table was our little kerosene lamp. At the base where the flame gleamed, I saw a brilliant cross, but at the top, around the crinkled edge, I saw a sparkling crown. Then I saw the lovely figure of my Lord. His hand was stretched out to me. Oh, how sweet was His face!
>
> "If you take the cross, you can have the crown," He said. I had been asked to go to Taiping and I was thinking about it. All the difficulties came to my mind.
>
> "Lord, your cross is too heavy for me to bear," I responded. I could not say yes.
>
> The vision changed. The room was cold and desolate. His presence was gone. My heart was lonely and sad.
>
> "Oh, Lord, forgive me," I cried. "Speak to my heart again." A second time the gracious presence of the Lord filled the room and He said as before, "If you'll take the cross, I will give you the crown." Strangely, my heart was flooded with fears and I cringed. "Oh, Lord, Your cross is too heavy for me. I can't take my family to Taiping."

Once again, my Lord was gone. Once again, my heart was deeply grieved. If only I had one more opportunity to hear His voice, I would not fail Him again. Sorrow filled my breaking heart. Would He come again?

Strange but true, there stood my precious Jesus in all His beauty and glory. Oh, how I loved Him. His face was sad and His eyes pleading.

"Take my cross and you can have My crown." Once again the powers of darkness assailed me with greater fury than ever before. I could not answer—my lips were dumb. My Lord waited and waited. Then, with deeply piercing eyes full of love, He looked into mine and said, "My grace is sufficient for you."

"Yes, Lord, I'll take Your grace for the cross You give." A wonderful peace and joy filled my whole being.

As Gerhard finished reading the account he dropped to his knees. "Now Lord, once again You are asking me to make a hard decision. We have struggled and suffered in Taiping. Now others will reap where we have planted. But, precious Lord, I am willing for Your will, if only I may have the joy of Your presence."

Alma stirred. Gerhard embraced her tightly.

"I have just given up the work in Taiping," he said quietly.

"I'm glad you settled it, honey. Whatever you decide is fine with me. There is still much work for us to do in the villages around Datong, you know."

The city of Datong was busy preparing for the Chinese New Year and the church was organizing their upcoming evangelistic meetings. At the Mission house Grandma and Alma were counting diapers for the day when "another little missionary," as Gerhard called the baby, would arrive.

"I would have felt better if we had left everything and gone to Wuhu for the birth of this baby," he complained one day late in January when Alma's labor pains began.

"Maybe we should have, but things went so well with Bette that I feel confident about this one. We'll trust the Lord again, honey." Alma's face was pale, her breathing difficult.

Grandma and Gerhard had made all the preparations for the home birth. As the hours dragged on, Gerhard became anxious and sent a telegram to Wuhu asking the doctor to come. He could make it in seven hours, he replied, if he caught the right boat. But would he come? And, if he did come, would he be able to save the mother and child?

Gerhard did not want Alma to see how frantic he felt. Rather than sit and watch her suffer through the labor pains, he went downstairs to his study. No sooner had he arrived, than he heard a voice.

"Come quickly, Gay. Alma is asking for you," Mother Sarah called.

Gerhard bounded up the stairs and knelt by the bed.

"I can't see, Gay, nor hear. Pray for me." Alma's voice was weak. Gerhard reached for her hand and held it tightly.

"Oh, God," he prayed earnestly, "spare my wife and baby."

Cloth footsteps sounded on the stairs.

"The Chinese lady doctor from across the river is at the gate," called Mrs. Li.

"Oh, thank you," replied Gerhard, his face twisted with apprehension. "Mrs. Jacobson is very bad. Pray that the Lord will spare her and the baby's life."

"Trust God, dear pastor," responded Mrs. Li, her sweet smile bringing a moment of relief.

It didn't take the young doctor long to assess the situation. She administered a stimulant and within minutes Grandma could see the color returning to her daughter's cheeks. The doctor bent over Alma to examine her.

"The baby is coming," she announced. Everyone leaped into action and before long, cries of the newborn blended with grateful praise to the Lord.

"You sure gave us a scare and your mama a hard time, little girl," Gerhard said picking up the little bundle in the blanket.

The girls were up early the next morning.

"Come and see your little sister," Grandma said, taking them into the next room where Evelyn Marie slept in a white wicker basket.

"We heard the cats crying last night," Doris told her daddy.

"No, that was the baby you heard crying," he laughed.

"Where did she come from?" chorused the trio.

"An angel brought her from heaven," Alma responded, smiling weakly.

The three peered at the little red wonder in the basket.

"Why didn't you call us when the angel came so we could see it?" Winnie scolded.

"Maybe next time," Alma promised.

The Shantzes, along with David and Mary Olson, picked up the responsibilities in Taiping. The Olsons were expecting their first child after several years of waiting. Mrs. Olson and Alma had many things in common and a deep bond existed between them. Yes, there was something special about this young missionary woman.

"When your time arrives for the baby," Alma advised Mary one day, "please be sure to go to Wuhu. This is your first and you can't tell how it will go, you know."

"Oh, yes," said Mary Olson. "We've made arrangements with Dr. Brown already. I'm sure nothing will happen unless it comes unexpectedly."

Several months passed and with each passing day no news was good news. Evidently all was going well with Mary and her baby.

What a glorious spring! Alma thought one day as she took the blankets from the railings of the upstairs veranda. A good airing always made them smell sweet and fresh.

That night Alma woke Gerhard.

"I can't sleep. I feel something has happened in Taiping. I'm worried about Mary Olson. Let's pray for them." As she prayed Alma began to sob. "Oh, Lord, please watch over Mary and spare her life, if it be Thy will."

The next day, Wang arrived at the back door, a telegram in his hand, his face grim.

"Mary Olson and baby with Jesus. David Olson," it read.

The dragon had struck again.

15

The Dragon's Work: Qingyang

Qingyang (CHING yahng), the Jacobsons' assigned city, nestled at the foothills of the lofty Yellow Mountains, home of the fierce Chinese tiger. An ancient, seven-arched stone bridge crossed the narrow, turbulent river winding through the valley. And from the river, hundreds of black-tiled roofs stretched as far as the eye could see.

In the distance, rivaling Mt. Fuji for beauty, Qingyang's Pencil Peak rose above the white petals of lotus-like clouds and stood guard over the city.

Missionary work in Qingyang had never been easy. After the early years of blessing, unfortunate events began to take place. It was rumored that the Mission property was haunted.

And a pastor's wife committed suicide by hanging herself from the rafters of the parsonage. Demonization became common among new converts.

Buddhist homes in the city boasted six-inch high clay figures which represented the tortures of the Buddhist purgatory and hell—people's bodies being sawn asunder by demons, others having their tongues pulled out or being burned with hot irons or eaten by demons—and even worse tortures.

The Mission compound in Qingyang had been looted after the 1927 uprising when anti-foreign elements destroyed foreign-owned properties all across China. So neighboring Alliance missionaries Mary Baer and Lida White crossed the hills from Taiping to help Alma and Gerhard clean up the debris. Dishes that had been buried under the banana trees were dug up, and each day more valuables were returned by the Christians. Gradually the Jacobsons settled down to regular missionary activities—regular except for the evangelistic forays into neighboring Qimen (CHI mun) and the tragic events at the MK school.

Because the Qingyang church was thirty years old and well-established, Gerhard and Pastor Sha decided to focus on outstation ministries. The first series of meetings would be held in the isolated city of Qimen. The enemy was not pleased with the plan.

One night, Gerhard and Alma left the younger girls, Bette and Evey, in the Mission house close by while they attended a meeting at the church.

During the evening, Bette got up to use the chamber pot.

"Bette, is that Daddy looking at us in his bathrobe?" Evey asked in a trembling voice.

"No, it isn't Evey," Bette screamed as her eyes fixed on a hideous, leering figure standing in the bedroom doorway. Bette jumped back into bed and both girls hid under the covers.

When Gerhard and Alma came home, Bette asked, "Daddy, why did you come into our room and make such a terrible face to scare us?"

Gerhard looked at the frightened girl.

"I wasn't home all evening, honey," he finally responded. "I was at the church just across the yard."

Recognizing this incident to be an attack of the enemy, the Jacobsons knelt by the girls' bed and pleaded for the house and all in it to be covered with the precious blood of the Lord Jesus Christ. After that prayer, there were no more strange occurrences.

The meetings at Qimen were especially blessed of God. Over fifty people actually stayed on the compound and many others attended the evening services. The Holy Spirit revealed sin and there was deep confession and repentance.

The hot months were fast approaching—the time to go to the mountains. Before their extended furlough, Gerhard and Alma had talked about wanting to build their own cottage at Jigongshan. But since the missionary allowance was just $50 per month, Gerhard could not see how it would be possible. However, Matthew Birrel had not only offered the lot next to his house—on a rocky slope where the best rocks could be saved for the foundation—but he had lent Gerhard $500 with which to build the house. Now, three years later, the Jacobsons would finally see their new home.

At the bottom of the hill, the family stepped out of the sedan chairs and climbed a narrow footpath snaking around a giant maple. They rested under its branches to catch a breath before heading for the summit. Suddenly, as they reached the ridge, the house came into view.

Constructed of gray brick and sparkling granite, it nestled into the side of a yellow granite hillside. A sturdy retaining wall held back the sandy soil of the wide front yard with its clumps of flaming red and yellow flowers.

The carriers wearily dumped the baggage in front of the stone pillars supporting the porch. Extracting carrying poles and ropes from the mounds of baggage, they grumbled about the steep climb and wiped their sweaty faces with long, blue-linen turbans.

Gerhard carefully counted out each man's wages into his hand. They stared in stony silence until he produced the silver dollar tip. Then they smiled and bowed, delighted at the generosity (or was it stupidity?) of the foreigner who gave them so much, along with pieces of gospel literature.

The Birrels had opened and cleaned the house for them. And the Hansons with their four children were already on the mountain as well. This would be an enjoyable summer— good fellowship, cool mountain breezes and the cool water in the Jigong pool. Much of Alma's time would be occupied with labeling and preparing clothes for Doris and Winnie to enter the American School there that fall.

All too soon the summer came to an end and Gerhard and Alma once again said tearful goodbyes to the girls. Perhaps it was God's mercy that none of them could predict the events of the year that lay directly ahead.

Gerhard and Alma were hardly back home in Qingyang when news came that Chiang Kai-shek army and the communists were clashing in the province surrounding Jigong mountain. Various cities and towns had been captured and destroyed by the Red Army. And soldiers often passed back and forth near the school. Their proximity soon became a source of concern for the faculty who feared that they or even some of the children might be captured and held for ransom. Rumor had it that on one occasion the communists had planned to attack the school, but hearing that there were only women and children there and little food and money, they concluded it was not worth the effort.

Although the year passed uneventfully, the Jacobsons and other parents thought it would be wiser either to put their children in another school or teach them at home the following year. Gerhard and Alma made a tough decision—to send their girls to the Shanghai American School. This time they would rent a house and Alma would stay with the children. Gerhard would remain in Qingyang and manage the station work. The Mission affirmed the plan.

Three months passed before Gerhard visited his family in Shanghai. The political situation around Jigong was much improved, he reported, and some missionaries were taking their children back to the mountain. Once again, with their hearts and minds torn, Alma and Gerhard had to make a decision. This time they decided to send Doris and Winnie back to Jigong after Christmas. But Jigong did not prove as safe a place as had been predicted nor as the Jacobsons had hoped.

One evening, unexpectedly, the generator turned off. The children assumed it was the usual overload until one of the teachers came to the study hall.

"You are all to go to the dormitory as quietly as possible," she whispered.

Once at the dormitory, they were told to go to their rooms and to put a change of clothes, a loaf of bread and a tin of milk in their laundry bags and to get a blanket and return to the supervisor's room. They would wait there together for the signal to start hiking down the mountain.

But the anticipated signal never came. When the children got tired, they were sent back to their rooms with orders to sleep with their clothes on.

The next morning everything seemed under control on the mountain and all the children were still there. The high school boys had been at lookout forts all night to serve as a warning if communist soldiers were sighted coming up the mountain. They saw nothing.

However, the following day word arrived that Bert Nelson, a young Lutheran missionary, had been captured. On the heels of this announcement came the news that Kristoffer Tvedt, the father of Winnie's roommate, Tulla Tvedt, had also been taken and was being held for ransom.

A few days later, the school moved.

That spring Winnie wrote a letter to her parents. It read in part:

> Dearest Mother, Daddy, Bette and Evey;
> I like my new teacher Miss Alice Anderson very much. She teaches us music and drawing. I want to tell you that I know I am saved. Other kids

were saying they didn't know if they were saved or not. But Anabel Schlosser said that she knew she was. One Sunday afternoon when I was alone reading my Bible in my bedroom I read First John 5:13-14. It says we can know we are saved if we believe in Jesus. I do believe, so now I know I am saved. My teacher corrected my spelling and the periods.
Love, Winnie.

P.S. Tulla's mother and her new baby sister are here in Hankow. I like to visit them and watch them give the baby a bath. We pray for Tulla's daddy every day that he will be released.

Meanwhile, during a second evangelistic journey to Qimen, Gerhard and Alma once again faced a decision.

"Here we are doing pioneering work again, Alma," Gerhard said one evening, a big smile breaking across his face. "How do you like it? Do you think we could move here to Qimen? I'd be glad to stay here. How about you, honey?"

Alma thought a moment.

"Yes, this would be a thrilling place to work. It's been nine years since missionaries were here. That's why the people are so open. Perhaps, just perhaps, we can move here in the fall."

Half a dozen wars were raging in North China. The Chinese looked on helplessly as Japan carried out a lightning occupation of Manchuria, followed by an attack on Shanghai.

Flooding of the Yangtze River also affected 50 million people, and to crown it all, the nationalists, Chiang Kai-shek's forces, failed to defeat the communists who were overflowing into the neighboring provinces around Qingyang. Wherever the communists went, hundreds of civilians, including Christians, died—victims of the Red terror. It would be three years before it would be safe for missionaries to spend their summers on Jigong Mountain.

That fall the Jacobsons moved to Qimen.

16

The Dragon's Fangs: Qimen

The clouds on the horizon turned crimson and gold as Gerhard left the Mission lot and made his way through the darkening city to their rented quarters. The walls of the Qimen Mission house were almost up and the carpenters had spent the day putting in windows and doors. Gerhard planned to reserve this evening to talk to one of the magistrate's men, an army officer. *What can I say to lead him to the Lord?* he prayed as he walked.

That evening, after the officer had poured out his sin- and pain-filled story, he sobbed, "Oh, Pastor Jacobson, I would gladly give my right arm if only I could have my sins forgiven."

"But you don't have to give your right arm!" Gerhard assured the man. "Look, here it says in God's Word that Jesus gave all that was needed—that was Himself. He died on the cross to pay for your sins. Can you believe that? Can you believe that He loves you in spite of your past?"

"Oh yes! I can and I do."

The young officer and the missionary knelt in prayer and the officer poured out his confession to the Lord with many tears. Gerhard marveled at the number of the magistrate's men who were finding Christ. None of them, including Gerhard himself, knew then that for many it was to be their last chance.

Alma and the Bible woman spent many fruitful hours in the homes around Qimen. Among those who came to Christ was a woman named Mrs. Fong who accepted the Lord against the wishes of her husband.

"Sen Semu (SEN Seh MOO), Mrs. Pastor," the Bible woman exclaimed breathlessly one day as she rushed into the Mission house in search of Alma, "you'll never believe what has happened to Mrs. Fong."

"No, what happened?" Alma asked.

"She poisoned her husband. No, I mean he poisoned himself."

"Just a minute," said Alma. "What really happened? Let's sit down and start from the beginning."

"Well," the woman stopped for breath, "Mr. Fong bought some poison on the street—to kill the rats in his house, he claimed. But he was so angry that his wife became a Christian he really intended it for her.

"When Mrs. Fong put the rice into their bowls for dinner yesterday and went into the kitchen for the vegetable dish, he mixed some poison into her bowl. Just before she sat down, he excused himself, not wanting to watch her eat the poisoned rice.

"While he was gone, Mrs. Fong bowed her head to pray before eating. When she finished there was a big spider in her bowl. She brushed it off and exchanged bowls with her husband. After she finished eating and had gone into the kitchen, her husband returned and ate his rice and vegetables. She heard his screaming a few moments later and found him writhing on the floor. Before he died, he confessed everything to his wife."

This incident turned out to be the breakthrough that Gerhard and Alma were looking for in the city of Qimen. In the year that followed, many of the gentry and wealthier class responded to the gospel and prepared for baptism. More opportunities than ever opened for the Jacobsons to share the good news.

In the countryside, however, the enemy of the souls of men was still doing his best to hinder God's work. Everywhere there were rumors of communists and bandits roaming the county. Poverty-stricken citizens and criminals gladly joined up with them to "solve" the problems of empty rice bowls and hungry stomachs.

Alma and Gerhard had known for several weeks that the communists were active in the south and west. On several occasions, they had even threatened the city, but the magistrate urged the missionaries not to leave as it would create a panic. The national government, seemingly oblivious to the situation or too weak to confront it, sent no soldiers. And the local police and militia were few in number. There was no doubt in anyone's mind that the city of Qimen was vulnerable.

"Evangelist Hu is here," Gerhard announced one day. "I think it would be a good time to introduce him to the magistrate and his officers."

"I think you're right, Gay," Alma agreed. "Even though the magistrate doesn't think it is a good time to have public meetings, we can meet in our downstairs chapel. What about having the magistrate in for a feast?" A feast was always good for public relations!

"The sooner the better so we can get started with the meetings," Gerhard replied.

What a feast it was! The magistrate, looking owlish in his heavy, dark-rimmed glasses and silks, partook generously from each dish as did his twelve military companions. The evening seemed to be going well until part way through the meal a runner from the *yamen* rushed in to say that there was an urgent telephone message for the magistrate.

The magistrate excused himself from the table. Some moments later when he returned to the feast, his face was ashen.

"Pastor and Mrs. Jacobson," he announced in solemn tones, "please excuse us. The communists are only a few miles away from the city. We must get our wives and children out as soon as possible."

Gerhard rose from the table, his rice bowl in his hand.

"Gentlemen," he said firmly, "a wise man will make a great matter into a small matter, then he will make a small matter into nothing at all. Please continue to eat. We must not rush out or the people of the city will know there is trouble and panic will ensue."

Gerhard's admonition brought some calm to the situation, but little by little the men left one after the other. Finally the magistrate himself got up to leave.

"Sen Mushe," he said, turning to Gerhard, "go as quickly as possible. Leave by the back streets, and don't take anything with you."

The Jacobsons decided to take his advice.

Packing only a few suitcases and a bed roll, Gerhard and Alma put their silverware in a satchel and stole out of the house. It was raining, but the chair bearers were willing to travel with the promise of extra pay. Memories rushed through their minds as they made their way through the silent, darkened streets. *Could God be taking them away just as the gospel was beginning to penetrate the area? Had they suffered through the birth pangs of a Church for nothing? Was this part of His plan? Would they ever be back?*

The answers were soon evident.

As the party entered the mountain pass, they took one last look back down the valley. Qimen was in flames.

The news from Qimen the next day was disturbing. Stores had been looted and burned, their wealthy owners horribly tortured and killed. The military were caught. Many of the young officers who had recently come to Christ were slain. The one bit of good news was that God had spared the life of the magistrate and his family.

With heavy hearts, Alma and Gerhard proceeded to Qingyang. But nowhere seemed safe for foreigners in this big land. In May, the communists raided a city where a young Alliance couple, the Howard Smiths, worked. Howard was captured. Gerhard wrote home:

> Dear Mother and Sister Ann,
> We are asking our churches in the homeland to unite with us in prayer for the release of Howard Smith. You will remember that we prayed for the Lutheran missionary, Mr. Tvedt, and he was released, although Bert Nelson died in captivity. Last year Henry Ekvall, the son of the Ekvalls you know so well, was captured and his body thrown down a well. The communists were tipped off that he was carrying money for the Standard Oil Company. These men can be very bloodthirsty. But as you pray, God can do miracles, I'm sure.
> Lovingly, your son and brother, Gay.

After two months in captivity Howard managed to escape from the communists only to fall into the hands of spirit-soldiers. These vicious men believed that strangers who wandered into their territory were devils. Only by allowing them to believe that he was a Russian did they let him go. They feared Russian retaliation if they killed him. It was a great day of victory when Howard came hiking up the mountain at Jigong.

It was Christmastime. Alma and Gerhard mourned the loss of many items of personal value destroyed in the attack on Qimen, but they rejoiced with the news that the Christians were standing firm. The communists were now in all counties north of the river and were even now infiltrating south into their county.

December 9—a day to be remembered. Alma was airing bedding and Gerhard was busy with his bees.

"I can hardly wait for the girls to come home," Alma told Gerhard. "I'm going to bake a special cake with raisins, dried persimmons and the candied orange peel I made."

No sooner had she gotten the words out of her mouth than heavy footsteps pounded across the front porch and the door burst open.

"*Ai-ya, ai-ya*, Sen Mushe, Sen Semu! The news, it is terrible!" The gatekeeper was standing before them, his face contorted.

"Yes, tell us. What is it?" Gerhard asked anxiously.

"Our nearest missionary neighbors, the Stams, have been killed by the communists. They were beheaded yesterday. Only their baby daughter is alive." The gatekeeper began beating his breast and crying uncontrollably.

John and Betty Stam? Their China Inland Mission neighbors? Dead? Beheaded? Gerhard and Alma could hardly believe it. The Shas were also on the porch. Everyone was talking at once.

"You must get ready to leave immediately," Pastor Sha told the Jacobsons. "The communists are very close. Don't bother to close the house. We will take care of everything for you."

The next morning Gerhard and Alma joined hundreds of other pitiful refugees choking the road from Qingyang to Datong. Communist flags could already be seen blowing in the breeze on the surrounding hillsides.

"Will this be our last time to see Qingyang and Qimen?" Gerhard asked his wife as they marched stiffly but slowly, pressed along by the crowd.

Alma looked at her husband. There was no answer to his question. Only God knew what the future held. For now they were lost in their own thoughts.

Christmas that year was celebrated at the headquarters compound of Wuchang. It was there that Gerhard and Alma learned what had actually happened to the Stams. They had just recently settled in their new assignment at Tsingteh (CHING deh), Anhui province, when a unit of 2,000 communist soldiers suddenly attacked the city. With no warning of impending danger, the missionaries were easily captured and led toward a nearby village.

As they were being marched down the road, a Christian farmer begged for the life of Priscilla, their baby. The answer came back, "Your life for hers." With the flash of a soldier's sword, the farmer's head was cut off.

The next morning, December 6, 1934, John and Betty and a Christian doctor were bound and taken out of the village. At the top of a small hill, they were ordered to kneel. Then, surrounded by a jeering crowd, they calmly bowed to the executioner's knife. Their baby, left in a house in the village, was later discovered and rescued by some Christians who took her to Wuhu.

Six months later, the Jacobsons were on the high seas, sailing to America for their second furlough. Would they some day return to their beloved Anhui province? The answer remained to be seen.

Still, amidst war and bloodshed, the Church in China, the Pearl—was being formed.

17

The Dragon Attacked: Shanghai

A Haunted House. Smallpox. "Baby Boy" Jacobson.

Sitting on her deck chair, Alma stared at the words on the note paper in front of her. She was trying to get a few ideas for messages she would be called on to give on furlough.

It was hard to think about sermon topics when the family was having such a good time on shipboard. But she knew her time would be at a premium once they were settled back in the U.S.

A "Haunted House." Well, that referred to the Jacobsons' new home at Jigong. Memories flooded Alma's mind.

Bette, then twelve years old, had been given the best upstairs room. It was facing west and had a nice big window. So, Gerhard and Alma were surprised when she gave it up to Winnie. Then, after some weeks passed, Winnie let Doris have the room.

Within days, Doris came to breakfast with an almost unbelieveable story about things flying around the room in the night. A "heavy one," she said, had pounced on her bed. Bette and Winnie also told about waking up feeling a threatening presence in the room. They couldn't go back to sleep, they said, unless they sang and prayed.

"We can't have this in a house that belongs to the Lord," Gerhard announced. He and Alma went upstairs and, praying for the blood of Jesus Christ to cover their home and all who were in it, they cast out any evil spirits who might have taken up residence. From that time on, the girls slept in the room undisturbed.

"Smallpox" referred to an incident which had taken place when Gerhard and Alma escaped from Qimen to live in their Jigong home. One day while Gerhard was fixing the stoves for the winter, Doris came back from school with the news that a primary school student, Mary Ann Johnson, was very ill. Nobody thought too much about it until a doctor was brought from a nearby town to take care of her.

Soon the news came that Mary Ann had smallpox and everyone would have to be vaccinated. The next information arrived several days later while the children were in a science class.

The teacher was called out, and in a few minutes returned, looking agitated and mumbling something under his breath. The students, in the middle of their experiment, paid little attention.

Then the teacher cleared his throat.

"I said, 'Mary Ann is gone.'"

"Baby Boy Jacobson." One May day Gerhard was sitting across the breakfast table from his wife.

"What is it, darling?" he asked anxiously, looking at her pale complexion.

"I'm afraid I'm going to lose my baby, Gay. I think we'd better make a hurried trip to the Wuhu hospital."

Within two days Alma was at the emergency room at the Methodist Hospital. The baby, their sixth, arrived prematurely and lived only a few hours.

"Oh, Gerhard," Alma cried as the shock of the news gripped her heart, "I'm so sorry. We waited for a boy so long."

Even now, as Alma sat on the deck of the ship, the pain and the tears were still there. But, yes, she could share that too with the women in America. They would understand her loss.

In the early days the John Woodberrys had begun a thriving work for the Alliance in the Hongkew (Chinese) district of Shanghai. After their retirement, their daughters Ora and Ethel carried on the work. Both were ten years older than Gerhard and Alma.

Ethel, a victim of childhood polio, relied on crutches to get around. Her radiant spirit and excellent Bible teaching made her a favorite with students. Ora's shining gray hair and gracious face and manner were eclipsed only when she sang and accompanied herself at the piano. The spiritual leadership of both women was indisputable.

Behind the church a beautiful, large compound contained two three-story buildings which served as an elementary school and residences for missionaries, teachers and workers.

The Jacobsons, returned from furlough, felt right at home there but missed the three girls who had traveled alone to the Jigongshan school and Doris who had stayed in the States to attend Asbury College.

Rumors of impending war were once again rearing their ugly head. This time, it appeared that the war would take on global dimensions. In Japan, factory assembly lines were rolling off weapons made from scrap iron obtained from the USA. In China, Chiang Kai-shek was contemplating the possibility of a strike by the Japanese. In the West, Hitler was boasting about the master race and belittling the Jews.

But living under such threats was not new to the Jacobsons. It seemed that their entire life had been lived in war.

As the summer heat once again blanketed Central China, the Jacobsons made their way to their home in Jigong. It would be good to leave the bustling metropolis of Shanghai for a little space and fresh air. They were also anxious to see the girls again.

Together around the supper table one night they chatted and laughed about the trip they had made across the United States during furlough—all six of them and their baggage piled into a second-hand, green Model A supplied by donations from friends and relatives. What fun it had been to visit their extended family and to see the sights they had only read or heard about.

"Not many families have that kind of hilarious trip together during the Depression," Gerhard told the girls as they ate their chicken and dumpling soup. "That was really a great privilege the Lord gave us, you know." Everyone agreed. The trip became one of the memories the family would treasure for years.

As they talked, a commotion could be heard outside. Evelyn ran to the window. A man was racing up the hill frantically waving a sheet of paper. Gerhard went to the door. As he opened it, an envelope was thrust into his hands.

"August 9, 1937—Jigong Radio News," the

note inside read. "A Japanese officer was accidentally shot near the bridge at the entrance to the Hongkew District of Shanghai. In retaliation, the Chinese city has been severely damaged by bombs. Several were accidentally dropped on the international settlement as well. Let us join in prayer for our suffering brethren."

Signed, Jigong Radio News

18

Confronted by the Dragon: On the Air

Images of the destruction leaped through Gerhard's mind. *The compound,* Gerhard thought. *Has anything happened to our compound? What about the caretaker and others? And what about our believers and friends in the international community?*

"I'll have to get back to Shanghai as soon as possible to see how our people and our property have fared," Gerhard told Alma and the girls. "We may have lost everything. I just hope no one was hurt or killed."

"Well, the war with Japan broke out a month ago in Beijing and look how many cities have already been taken over," Alma reminded him. "China isn't ready, but Japan won't stop until she has it all." It was true. Slowly but surely the armies of the Rising Sun were nibbling away at China's seacoast and gaining ground inland.

After Gerhard left, Alma and the girls packed up their trunks and headed off to Hong Kong where they would wait until the American consul allowed them to return to Shanghai.

In Shanghai, Gerhard found out that the Hongkew District, including the Mission compound, had been barricaded. But the Japanese were allowing trucks from the international community to help clear away debris and burn rubbish. A Christian truck driver, Mr. Langdon, was able to get an arm band for Gerhard so he could ride along.

"You go ahead and do your work," Gerhard told the driver as they bounced over the streets of Hongkew. "Leave me at the Alliance property on Szechuan Road (all the missionaries were by now in the international settlement) and when you've finished, pick me up."

"That's a bit dangerous, sir," the man replied. "No one is supposed to be prowling around the buildings. The Japanese don't care, you know. They will shoot first and ask questions later."

Despite the warning, when the vehicle came to a stop, Gerhard jumped out and opened the gate to the compound. Scrambling around broken glass and shattered bricks, he finally reached the building that onced housed the church.

What a mess! The garage door was gaping open. The still new black Ford V8 that had been such a help in Shanghai was gone. Crawling up the stairs to the trap door to the attic, Gerhard burst through a large bomb hole in the roof. *How sad!* he thought, pausing to survey the destruction. The roof was peppered with holes.

A bomb had also struck the church tower, leaving many of the beautiful stained-glass windows shattered. Gerhard crossed to the workers' apartments to assess the devastation there. Refrigerators, stoves, furniture, radios—anything of value—had been looted. Plaster and broken glass stuck to dishes and bedding. Rain and wind had spoiled what remained.

Suddenly Gerhard heard a shout. Rushing to the balcony, he came face to face with the barrel of a gun pointed directly at him. More from a gut reaction than a premeditated response, Gerhard shouted "hallelujah" as loudly as he could. The soldier turned and ran.

Gerhard walked into another room. On the wall was a motto: "Fear not: for I am with thee" (Isaiah 43:5, KJV). The wild beating of his heart slowed. "I've got to get this bedding and clothes together for our workers," he muttered to himself as he set about to collect everything that was salvageable. It appeared that the room that served as a warehouse for Alliance Press materials was the only one untouched by the devastation.

Soon Mr. Langdon returned and the men piled the truck high with precious, if somewhat soggy and stained, belongings. Slowly the vehicle pulled out through the gate.

"No, you . . . ," a guard shouted, pointing at Gerhard and poking a pile of Chinese garments. "No can take."

Glancing over his shoulder at a believer sitting in the back of the truck, Gerhard held up a hand for money. A dollar dropped into it.

"Mine, mine. I buy," Gerhard said emphatically. The shamefaced guard let them pass.

Gerhard fired off a letter to Alma and the girls in Hong Kong.

> Are you reading the newspapers about the atrocities of war? Nanking has fallen and the civilians were treated badly. Some were executed, some burned alive. Thousands of others were tied in bundles and used for bayonet practice. That and more is also happening in the Hongkew District. We suffer when we see our beloved Chinese suffer!
>
> At the Garden Bridge the sentries playfully prodded a man with their bayonets. One old man was beaten and thrown into the river while the Japanese soldiers laughed and cheered. I pray every day for our enemies so as not to hate them.
>
> I have found one of those narrow little houses in a complex inside a compound in the French concession of Shanghai. So, you all can come here after the Christmas break. You'll have to leave Evelyn in the hostel to finish her year at the British school, but Winnie and Bette can continue to study here. Let me know how soon I should come to Hong Kong to help pack.
>
> Love and kisses, Gay

Alma and the girls didn't know what to expect as their intercoastal vessel approached Shanghai and they entered the city. The first thing that greeted their eyes was the crowds of beggars and refugees riding on carts, bicycles, sedan chairs and every other possible form of conveyance. Some were still weeping. Many had trudged miles leaving their bombed-out towns and villages, hoping each day to find work and food in Shanghai. The devastation was appalling.

The city constructed huts for the masses on the outskirts, but during the summer's heat, lack of water and sanitation brought death in epidemic proportions from cholera, dysentery and typhoid. Each morning the Shanghai Public Works Department sent trucks to scoop up the dead and bury them.

Winnie was looking out an upstairs window one afternoon when she saw a truck full of coffins pull into the vacant lot just over the wall. The carriers from the truck dug a wide trench and threw the coffins in, then drove away.

Then Winnie noticed that one carrier had been left behind—an indication that this was his last day of work. He sank to the ground beating his breast and crying out to the earth god to save his starving family.

At that moment the Lord asked Winnie if she was willing to give her life so the Chinese could hear about Jesus. Within only weeks she was standing on the deck of an ocean liner along with other classmates from the Jigong school, waving goodbye to her teary-eyed parents and sisters as she left for college in America.

Conditions continued to deteriorate. In December, a Japanese naval officer claimed he had received an order from Shanghai to clear the Yangtze River near Nanking of all shipping.

Immediately he sent up bombers. They circled above the three British warships and one U.S. warship, the *Panay,* docked there. Never dreaming of an attack, the sailors calmly gathered on deck. Within seconds, all were dead, killed by the bombs that rained down on them. Anti-aircraft came into action too late. The *Panay* sank with most of its crew.

"Why don't we declare war on Japan?" Americans in China were beginning to ask. Did President Roosevelt feel the country was not ready and the people would not rally behind him? All the U.S. demanded was reparations from Japan for their misdeeds, but the Jacobsons and many others could read the "handwriting on the wall." The view from their side of the ocean indicated that war was inevitable.

It was a cool crisp morning when Gerhard stepped outside the iron gate of their complex to the bus stop. His heart and mind were in a tumult. A fellow missionary, Mr. Lowe, was going on furlough and the well-to-do Christian businessman, K.S. Lee, had requested that Gerhard come to his office. He wanted to interview him, he said, about becoming the manager of Shanghai's Christian radio station XMHD.

Mr. Lee, tall and portly, welcomed Gerhard. As Mr. Lee explained his vision for the station and all the possibilities it afforded, especially in such a significant time in the history of China, Gerhard was challenged with the tremendous opportunities for sharing the gospel with the masses. He accepted the position on the spot. Time would reveal that this turn of events for the Jacobson family was engineered by God Himself.

In the months that followed Gerhard made many changes and the station grew in popularity. Famous American radio pulpiteers sent their messages to XMHD. Chinese and missionary evangelists and Bible teachers poured out their hearts in Spirit-anointed messages in Russian, English, Finnish, French and German. The response in monetary gifts and conversions was overwhelming.

Then Shanghai suffered another outrage of war—a wanton and deliberate air attack at midday when crowds were the heaviest. Three bombs rained down on the city, killing thousands. Broken, bleeding Shanghai. Millions without hope. Death, turmoil, chaos on every side. Surely this was the time to present the One who could bind up the brokenhearted and give hope to the hopeless.

"Let's have special meetings in the largest

auditorium in downtown Shanghai," Alliance evangelist Timothy Dzao suggested to Gerhard one day. "I believe the city is ready to hear God's Word." Gerhard knew the reputation of Timothy Dzao as a man of audacious faith. Perhaps this was a word from the Lord.

He paused only briefly.

"The biggest place would be on the top floor of the Sun Company," Gerhard responded. "It seats over a thousand."

"But can we afford to rent it?" Timothy asked. Then not waiting for an answer, he added, "Let's pray and believe God that we can." Gerhard decided to stand behind Timothy and do all he could to support him in this ambitious effort.

Announcements went out over the radio and every evening people crowded into the Sun Company auditorium until more than a thousand packed it out nightly. The Jacobsons enlisted the help of many Christian workers and missionaries to work with the inquirers and the follow-up program.

"Timothy Dzao certainly knows how to draw the net," Gerhard told the missionaries one week at their prayer meeting. "Now he wants to have time on the radio." The missionaries, including Alma, responded enthusiastically. Always a woman of prayer, she organized prayer chains throughout the city among the various Missions. And Pastor Dzao went on the radio.

Hardly daring to dream of a response, the evangelist invited those who wanted to make a personal commitment to Christ to come to the radio studio for prayer. At first they filled the reception room. Then they crowded into the recording room. When these rooms were filled with chairs, more were added in the halls. Finally even the halls could not hold the crowds and they sat on the stairways. It was a time of harvest. XMHD was experiencing its first radio revival.

But the Japanese were also aware of XMHD, particularly its news broadcasts which they threatened to disrupt with a buzzer. They tapped the office telephone and finally went so far as to send letters threatening Gerhard's life. He no longer answered either the doorbell or the telephone himself.

One afternoon the secretary took a call from a man with a heavy accent.

"He wants to speak to you," the secretary told Gerhand, "but he won't give any information about himself."

Gerhard picked up the receiver.

"Mr. Jacobson?" the voice asked.

"Speaking," replied Gerhard.

"Are you going to be in?"

"Yes, I'm in, but I'm on my way out," Gerhard answered warily.

"Just wait: I'll get you," the voice said. The line went dead.

Gerhard paced the floor like a caged lion.

What had those words meant? Should he go? Should he stay? What were the man's intentions?

A few moments later, a tall, powerfully built Indian Sikh strode into Gerhard's office. His right hand was tugging at his back pocket. *If it's the last thing I do, I'll knock that gun out of his hand,* Gerhard, still cautiously suspicious, thought to himself.

Then, with a deliberate gesture, the Sikh stretched out his hand. It contained a thick roll of bills. Gerhard could feel his muscles relax as he slowly reached for the gift. Carefully, he counted the money. There was $500 in Chinese currency!

"Take it all," the Sikh said, smiling, "I have been listening to your radio station every day and I want you to have this in appreciation for what it means to me and other Indians."

Gerhard took the policeman's big hand in his own and pressed it tightly. Tears streamed down the dark face and mingled with his beard as Gerhard talked to him about God's love. Then, abruptly, with a salute, the man slipped out the door.

One dark morning soon after the incident, Gerhard crept downstairs to pick up the paper and prepare the tea tray for Alma. He could hardly believe his eyes. The headline read: "Hitler expels Jews from Germany. Mercy ship with 500 aboard heads for Shanghai."

19

The Dragon Fights: The Rising Sun and the Swastika

Gray wisps of ocean fog wrapped around a thicket of bobbing junk sails and rows of massive buildings along Shanghai's deserted waterfront. Only a few straggling night workers on their way home joined Gerhard on the bus to the wharf where he would meet the first boatload of Jews.

As he stepped from the bus and walked briskly to the dock, rickshaws and food vendors silently moved past him in the fog. But Gerhard's mind was on other things, namely, the plight of these, God's chosen people.

At the dock, members of the Shanghai Jewish Relief Society were already holding up signs in German. Gerhard's eyes scanned the crowd.

He spotted John Quimby, a longtime friend and superintendent of the Shanghai Hebrew Mission.

"The mercy ship is bringing more than the number of Jews we anticipated and besides, each has ten pieces of baggage," Quimby told him. "Christians in Europe have paid these people's passage and given them a three-month living allowance."

"How many did you say are on this first ship, John?"

"There are supposed to be 500, but several hundred more crowded on board at the last minute. Now that Hitler's rage is full-blown, I predict the Jews will come by the thousands."

"I can't understand why China was the only country to open its doors to them," Gerhard responded, his voice nearly lost in the swirling wind.

"Oh, others were willing, but they required a sponsor who could guarantee an estate or annual income above $30,000 for each Jew. This ship even stopped along the way looking for a country that would change its policy."

Suddenly John looked up.

"Look, Brother Jake! There she is," he said, nudging Gerhard in the ribs.

A large white German liner with a red cross painted on its side was steaming up the river. Hundreds of faces could be seen peering over the rails as it pulled alongside the dock. The gangplank hit with a bang, but before any carriers could stream up its stairs, people rushed down like swarming bees.

Once on shore, they looked around blankly, too stunned to speak or cry out, like players in a tragedy, powerless to prevent the stroke of misfortune that had befallen them. From the decks, baskets, baby buggies, bundles and baggage of all kinds were handed down. And, on the pier, police and workers hustled the crowd along.

Shanghai had provided a number of large school campuses in the bombed-out Hongkew section of the city for the Jews. Committee members organized work crews to repair the roofing, floors, doors and windows as needed.

At their quarters, the Jews stared at the empty rooms and the Chinese who were carrying triple-decker bunks into them.

"Each room will accommodate forty-five couples," a burly German-speaking policeman announced to the crowd. "There is a dining room at the back of this building where you will be served today. By tomorrow you must organize yourselves into committees. Food will be sent to the camp, but you must cook and care for yourselves." Noisily people began to claim bunks and to pile their things on them.

That evening, John Quimby rode home with Gerhard. Alma set an extra place for him at the dinner table. Pulling out a chair, he shoved back a shock of white hair and sat down.

"We missed you today, Alma," he said, nodding his head vigorously as he spoke, "especially since you've always been so interested in our Jewish work."

"She hasn't slept well for nights, brother," Gerhard explained. "She worked so hard washing walls, doors and windows at our place in preparation for our first meeting with the Jews. Do you think we'll have much of a response to our invitation for Bible studies?"

"If we do, we can ask those who attend if they would like to move from that overcrowded building. One family to a room is a lot better than forty-five. You have at least fifteen rooms at the Szechuan Road property, don't you?"

"Yes, we do, John," Alma replied, smiling. "I'll be so happy to be in Jewish work once again."

Alma could hardly wait to tell her mother about this turn of events in their lives that brought back welcome memories of past days.

> Dear Mother,
> Yesterday, for the first time, we opened a meeting place for the Jews on Szechuan Road. We had a few Christians and thirty-six Jews. We whitewashed the school room and put up one of the Woodberry's stoves. It was cozy and warm.
> I played the organ and German hymnbooks were passed around. Tears rolled down the refugees' cheeks at the singing of "Ein Feste Berg ist Unser Gott" (A Mighty Fortress Is Our God). Mr. Rosenthal, a Christian Jew, who has been in a concentration camp and suffered greatly, exhorted his people to turn to Christ in their distress. Miss Jon, a German Swiss missionary, told them that although others despised and hated them, there

were many Christians who loved them and wanted to care for their needs. They were dumbfounded to learn that the Chinese Christians gave a generous offering for them last Sunday.

True to John Quimby's prediction, many mercy ships came to Shanghai until the number of Jewish immigrants from Germany rose to 10,000. Fifteen relief centers were opened in the Hongkew District and in the international settlement. Various relief societies and individuals provided money, clothes and food.

One day Gerhard received a phone call with the all-too-common news. A Jewess had succumbed to cholera due to lack of medicine and food. Would Gerhard hold the funeral?

"Lord, help me to use my imperfect Yiddish," he prayed as he left the office to hail a taxi.

When he arrived at the gate of the relief center, an agent from the center waved him to one side. With him was the undertaker. He hustled both of them and the husband of the dead woman to his long black hearse. The men climbed in on either side of the coffin.

Gerhard's eyes were riveted on the weeping man sitting beside him, a few artificial flowers clutched in his hand. Turning to the relief society agent, he said, "Let's stop at a florist shop and each buy a wreath for the casket. Can the Society afford that?"

Gerhard's companion nodded.

Finally the hearse reached the vacant lot the

city had recently reserved as a Jewish cemetery. Several carriers were standing around a freshly dug grave. Gerhard read from his German Bible and offered a brief message of comfort to the grieving man. Then it was over.

"Can you come to our home for supper?" Gerhard asked the bereaved husband. "My wife speaks better German than I do."

The man was quiet and withdrawn during the meal. But then, all of a sudden, in an explosive release of pent-up emotion, he began to tell his story.

"I was a successful young businessman in Germany," he began, "but when I fell in love and married a Christian, my family threw me out. My wife told me to trust in Christ many times but I refused. When we left Germany to come to China she wept bitterly. She didn't want to come, but because of her love for me she came. I loved her so much and now she is gone." The man's shoulders heaved as deep sobs burst from his heart.

" 'In my Father's house are many mansions' (John 14:2, KJV). Those are the words of the Lord Jesus," Gerhard responded in an effort to bring some solace to the man's brokenness. "Your wife is there now. Are you willing to receive her Savior as your Messiah?"

"Oh yes!" responded the Jew without hesitation. "You see, I have heard the gospel many times before, but in Germany I never saw such love for the Jews. When you and your friend bought fresh flowers for my wife's grave, I knew you loved me." He bowed his head. "It was the flowers that touched my heart," he repeated softly.

The days were busy for Alma and Gerhard. Never had Alma had so much work to do. Their home, in the western district of the international settlement of the city, welcomed hundreds of guests. Because of the increased pressures, Gerhard and Alma invited the Shas to come from Qingyang to help with the cooking and errands. The house also became a haven for missionaries passing through to Free China.

Gerhard held many positions including the chairmanship of the Mission which involved handling the funds for workers in the interior of Central China. Both Alma and Gerhard taught in a Christian school and in the fledgling Bible school. Many Jews believed in Jesus as their Messiah—Gerhard himself baptized seventy-nine. Despite the pressures, these were happy days for the family.

Another mild spring morning, Alma thought as she put on a rose-colored, short-sleeved jacket and skirt and picked up her satchel. Her mind, as she walked down the lane to the main gate of the compound, was on the fresh young faces of those she would be teaching in her English class.

Pulling up the latch, she glanced toward the

parked cars lining the street and stepped out. Suddenly, without warning, she found herself flying through the air. As she landed on the pavement, all went black.

At the Mission office, Gerhard was checking the Alliance Press books when the ring of a telephone broke the silence. He picked up the receiver. A woman was shouting and crying in Chinese.

"What, what! I can't understand. Talk slowly," Gerhard interrupted. Miss Marsh, the secretary, looked up from her desk.

"Yes, yes! Mrs. Jacobson, hit by a car? Where is she now? Don't cry. I'll be right there."

For a moment Gerhard felt faint.

"What's that? Alma hit by a car? I'll call a taxi. Just wait," Ethel Marsh ordered.

The taxi seemed to take forever to arrive and the ride seemed even longer. When it finally pulled up at the Jacobson's door, Gerhard sped up the stairs to the bedroom. Alma, small and white and still, lay on the bed. She smiled faintly.

"I feel fine, honey," she assured her husband. "Just a lot of pain right now."

"How did it happen?" asked Gerhard, handing her some aspirin and a glass of water.

"I don't really know, but the driver was the Russian who lives in the house on the corner. He was very distraught and carried me into the house. Really, Gay, don't look so worried. I'll be fine."

Despite Alma's assurances, Gerhard decided to call the doctor. An ambulance was sent to take her for X-rays.

"Your wife has ruptured her second lumbar vertebra," the doctor told Gerhard. "I'll do my best to strap her back but she must have three months bed rest. See that she sleeps with a board under her mattress."

The following weeks turned out to be a blessing in disguise. They provided a much needed rest for Alma.

Japan's invading army spread like black sludge across China. Generalissimo Chiang Kai-shek's capitol was moved to Chungking. Much of Central China was now under the Japanese, but the Alliance nationals and missionaries were in the west in Free China. Bombs fell daily on the cities and in the countryside. Special planes dropped supplies to missionaries cut off. Although the Chinese Task Air Force fought back, theirs seemed to be a losing battle.

American volunteers aided as they could. while General Chennault with his "Flying Tigers" bravely defended the Burma Road, China's only supply line.

The American consul at Shanghai warned everyone, particularly foreigners, that war with Japan was imminent and urged all women and children to leave. School would soon open again in Pyongyang, Korea where Evelyn was now attending, safely away from the war. Alma was worried about her being so far away and also about the other three girls in Wheaton, Illinois. Bette and Doris were studying at Wheaton College. Winifred had graduated from high school and had taken a job to save money for Bible school.

"I'm not sure I like Evelyn being so far away from us, Gay," Alma told her husband one day. "What if war breaks out and we're here and she's in Korea?"

Burdened with concern for all the girls, Alma set everything aside to spend a morning with the Lord. As she prayed she felt the Lord whisper the answer: "Go and make a home in the States for yourself and your daughters. They need you."

Gerhard agreed and events moved quickly. Gerhard, always frugal, decided that this might be their last chance to buy some Chinese things to take back to America. A new china shop had recently opened down on Nanking Road. Gerhard purchased a large set of delicate Bavarian dishes. Then going to a shop where camphor wood chests were carved, he ordered one large enough to hold the dishes along with some exquisitely embroidered linens picked out at another specialty shop. When Alma objected to the expenditure, Gerhard responded, "We don't know the future of China."

It was a dark, rainy night on November 18,

1940, when the *Empress of Asia* slipped her moorings from Shanghai's dock with Alma and Evelyn on board. A large crowd was on hand to see them off. The Jews kissed Alma's hand in appreciation for the love and care she had shown them.

Gerhard stood next to John Quimby.

"It was hard to see the girls leave China, one by one," Gerhard said, his voice breaking, "but it is a thousand times harder to say goodbye to one's wife. You've experienced it, I know, John." His wife had left Shanghai several years earlier for medical treatment in Canada, but died of a brain tumor before her husband was able to get to her side.

"To come home to an empty house—well, it's terrible, Jake," John whispered.

Both men stood in silence until the liner disappeared.

The following September, Doris and Winifred decided that the Nyack Missionary Training Institute was the place of God's leading for them. Once again, Alma turned to prayer.

"What would you think if we would all go to Nyack this year?" she asked the girls. By now, Doris had graduated from Wheaton College and Evelyn from Wheaton High School. The girls talked it over. Bette and Evelyn agreed to take a year at Nyack in order to become more grounded in God's Word.

The Alliance gave the family, which once again included Grandma Amstutz, rent-free use of Groff Cottage. *What a woman of faith!*, the Nyack people thought when Alma brought all four daughters to register. Much to everyone's surprise their entire tuition was paid by an unknown benefactor who had visited Shanghai and witnessed the Jacobson's ministry.

People could not understand Alma's serene spirit when month after month no word arrived from her husband. Transportation and communication in and out of Shanghai was virtually shut down.

While Alma was away on speaking tours, Grandma Amstutz cared for the girls. Everyone had jobs on the weekends and the Lord met their needs in a wonderful way.

By November of that year, when Japan realized that she needed to reopen diplomatic relations with the U.S., a delegation was sent to Washington to meet with President Roosevelt and Cordell Hull, the then Secretary-of-State.

The U.S. made it plain that Japan must withdraw from Indochina and China. But, on the 5th of December, Japan replied that these demands were unacceptable. President Roosevelt warned all the diplomats, both American and Japanese, that they should "give thought in this emergency to find ways of dispelling the dark clouds of war." Just how dark they were, was soon to become evident.

It was a bright Sunday morning, December 7. Grandma Amstutz, Alma and the girls had just returned from church when shouts were heard at their cottage door. It was Raymond Kowles, a former China missionary and classmate of Doris.

"Have you heard the news about Pearl Harbor?" he called.

20

The Dragon's Defeat: The Great Escape

The "bolt out of the blue" which had rocked the entire world only one day before now burst on the unwary citizens of Shanghai that terrifying Monday morning of December 8, 1941. The Japanese were bombing American and British warships in their own harbor.

Missionaries Ethel Marsh and Dorothy Dear rushed downstairs from their apartment to gather with Gerhard around the radio. Outside, bombs and bullets reeked havoc and sudden death. Japanese military tanks rumbled through the streets, firing on hapless people. Repeatedly a single command blared over the radio: "All Americans, British and foreign nationals remain indoors."

Feverishly, Gerhard twisted the dials of his radio tuning in to London, New York, Berlin and Calcutta. The Japanese, he found out, were also bombing Hong Kong, Manila, Singapore and Jakarta. But the worst attack had been on Honolulu where the U.S. fleet had suffered direct hits, with thousands killed.

Another twist and the dial struck a vastly different note. The strains of "Rock of Ages" pealed over the airwaves above the sound of booming guns. For Shanghai-landers it was the last message of Station XMHD, a message of peace in a world of war. Gerhard and the ladies bowed their heads in thanks to God for His safe retreat in a time of trouble.

The jangling of the telephone moved Gerhard to action. It was the voice of his secretary at the radio station.

"The Japanese are here and demand we go off the air. All other broadcasting stations have already closed down," she said, trying to maintain outward serenity.

"Keep on the air as long as you can," Gerhard's voice came back firmly.

"Ah-llo, Ah-llo," a man's voice yelled suddenly into the receiver. "Is this the manager of radio station XMHD?"

"It is."

"We cut station off air. We come get you. You stay home!"

Gerhard stared at the dead receiver in his hand, his mind a whirl. He turned to the ladies who were standing nearby.

"The Japanese are coming. You know they've always hated our news broadcasts. Maybe now they will take their revenge."

"We are going to pray that the Lord won't allow you to go to the 'bridge house,' " Ethel said in a choked voice. The bridge house had already become infamous as a place of torture.

"Only the Lord can save me, ladies," he reminded them as he handed Ethel the phone. She dialed the church, school and missionary residences as fast as she could, asking prayer for their leader.

Gerhard ascended the stairs to his room to gather a few articles of clothing into a suitcase. His thoughts were running wild. Visions of Japanese torture chambers filled his mind. He had gathered nothing when the doorbell rang. *Composure. That's what I need.* As he uttered a silent prayer, a deep, pervasive peace filled his being.

He would have been at the door in a moment but Wu Ma, Ethel's cook, opened it.

It was Lily Chen, the pastor's wife. In her hand was a bag.

"Look, we heard that the Japanese are coming for you. You can escape. Put on these clothes and come with me right away. We will leave the compound through the back wall. The church has made arrangements for you to travel with the pastor to Hangzhau. From there you will be smuggled into Free China. We have all the money you need. But you must come now!" she urged.

Gerhard stared at the women.

"Mrs. Chen, I thank you so much and the brethren of the Church. You know I handle all the funds for our Central China workers. How can I flee? Would I leave Miss Marsh and Miss Dear alone? I don't believe that would be the Lord's will for me, do you?"

"The Japanese wouldn't treat Miss Marsh as badly as they would you, I don't think," Mrs. Chen responded. "But you must do what you think best." She turned away sadly.

The door bell rang again. Wu Ma went to the door.

"Very sorry to disappoint you but the master of the house is not here," Wu Ma murmured, bowing deeply to the men.

"But you see he has returned," Gerhard interrupted, flashing a big grin as he stepped up to face the men.

The officer stared wide-eyed for a moment.

"You have a very loyal servant, Mr. Jacobson," he said.

The men seated themselves in the parlor. Gerhard recognized one of them to be Mr. Wauki with whom he had once had a rather unpleasant encounter.

Mr. Wauki had warned Gerhard several times that his radio broadcasts were clearly heard on the nearby Japanese-controlled islands and that they were lowering the morale of the people. *Can or will that encounter affect the events of the next few moments?* Gerhard wondered.

Suddenly, the leader of the group sat up straight.

"Mr. Jacobson, are you anti-Japanese?" he asked sharply.

Gerhard bowed his head slightly and offered a quick prayer for wisdom. He knew he must not say anything unwise or offensive.

"No, gentlemen," he smiled, "but naturally, I am pro-Ally." The response seemed to satisfy the group for the moment. Then, after further discussion, the men turned to Mr. Wauki.

"Tell us, what is your opinion of Mr. Jacobson? You know him!" they queried.

Gerhard held his breath. Would the man be his friend or foe? Minutes seemed to pass. Mr. Wauki finally cleared his throat.

"I think Mr. Jacobson is quite all right," he said flatly.

The men stood up slowly and filed out as Mr. Wauki apologized for "disturbing" Mr. Jacobson.

With the door safely closed, the two lady missionaries ran down the stairs laughing and crying for joy and, together with Gerhard and the servants, joined in an impromptu praise service.

Gerhard wrote to Alma:

Two days after Pearl Harbor, all foreigners were instructed to queue up for registration at Hamilton House. I stood in line all day. After that we began to queue up many times for many reasons. The first was to register lists of furniture and everything in our houses. The Japanese came and examined our homes, sealing every item.

Businesses, schools and churches have been forced to reorganize and submit to Japanese supervision. Japanese replaces all other languages. Pastors have to submit copies of their sermons to Japanese superiors before they are preached.

The hardest thing is the lack of transportation as all the gasoline was shipped to Japan. Bicycles and rickshaws replace cars and buses. The price of a bicycle has risen from $35 to $2,000 this year. Puppet money is used instead of the Chinese *yuan* or dollar.

I shall never forget the first time I stood in line at the bank. The line was four blocks long and it was not until closing time that I arrived at the window, only to have it shut in front of me! I saw Japanese trucks taking away loads of bank notes. Seventy-five percent of our money is confiscated.

Every day guerrilla war tactics are in operation. Shooting and hand grenade throwing are daily occurrences. Immediately after, that section of the city is blocked off until the offender is caught and killed. Most of us have had to keep food and money in several places in order not to starve as some have.

But now for the brighter side of things in Shanghai. There are two verses of Scripture that are so helpful to me. The first, Psalm 115:12, "The LORD hath been mindful of us" (KJV). He has not failed us in the past and He will not in the future. The second says, "My grace is sufficient for you" (2 Corinthians 12:9).

I go to the Alliance publishing office every day or meet at the church to encourage our Chinese brethren in prayer.

One evening I was caught there during an air raid which made it late when I started for home. I planned to catch a rickshaw on the next street when I saw a man following me. Under the street light I could see he had a hard face. Many times people have been mugged, robbed and killed on this street. So I sent an urgent prayer heavenward. Then I thought, *Two can play this game.* I hid in a doorway, then rushed out at him as he passed. "Hey," I said, "can't you see I'm on this side of the street? You get over to your side!" I think the poor fellow was so shocked to see a white face that he ran away terrified.

I want you to know that we have much to be thankful for, such as our liberty to come and go and the use of our radio and telephone. We can attend church and visit friends. Buying food is the most time-consuming activity as we must queue for it.

Now a personal note. I love you so much and would give anything in the world just to be with you and tell you so. I have your picture under the glass on my desk and sometimes I talk to you. Keep trusting, honey! Some day, God willing, we will be together again.

Love, Gay

21

The Dragon's Defeat: Together at Last

On February 8, 1943, Gerhard's telephone rang. An American, speaking in a low bass voice, said, "Be ready for internment on February 15. Meet at the city drill hall. You are allowed three pieces of heavy baggage: one should be a bed. The city express will pick these up and take them to the Pootung Prisoner Camp across the river. You will be allowed as much hand baggage as you can carry. Take food for two days. It is a camp for single or detached men."

"Thank you, sir," Gerhard answered courteously. "I'll be ready."

Gerhard put his head down on his desk. It had been two years since Alma and Gerhard had been together. Now, who knew how many more years it would be, if ever?

"Oh, Lord," Gerhard cried, "is this Your birthday present to me?" In just a week, on February 15, he would be fifty-four years old.

It was a bright sunny day when Gerhard, in a rickshaw nearly smothered by four suitcases, was swept along the streets. He was not alone. Rickshaws all around him were full of men with baggage heading to the city drill hall.

There they faced yet another queue—queues were becoming a way of life for Gerhard and thousands of other Shanghai residents. This time they were being asked to register (again) and receive their red armbands.

That done, the parade of prisoners headed, bags in hand, for the dock. On both sides of the streets Chinese waved and cheered.

The launch was jammed with far more passengers than it could safely hold. Finding a place to sit was well nigh impossible. Finally Gerhard caught sight of a friend.

"Where are they taking us, Willis?" Gerhard asked the former manager of the Christian Book Room.

"I'm told we're going to the British and American Tobacco Warehouse, a building that was condemned twenty years ago," Willis replied with a twinkle in his eye. "You know—condemned men, condemned building!"

Fortunately for the 1,500 men who assembled there, food was supplied and cooked that first day by the crew of the Dollar Liner ship, the *President Harrison*. It had been seized several days previously as it docked in Shanghai, its men and supplies brought to this camp.

Camp life was an adjustment for all. Each person was allotted an eight-foot square sleeping space. Jail birds, drug users, bums and beachcombers found themselves together with bank managers, doctors, lawyers, professors, businessmen and missionaries. Several hundred crew members from the *President Harrison* added to the spicy mixture. The variety of nationalities made communication difficult.

The next day the Japanese gave the men reject lumber from burned- or bombed-out buildings. Cubicles were hastily erected and camp life began to take on the monotonous routine of morning and evening roll call and the ever-present daily lectures by the camp supervisors.

"You will be given one pint of water each day and that is all," the Japanese commandant began his lecture. "You must organize yourselves in committees for self-government. You will have to cook, clean and care for this camp as you want it. Each person will be given a list of rules and anyone breaking them will be severely punished. No radios will be allowed. Now the name of this camp is 'Our Happy Home.' "

Committees were formed as quickly as possible. There were the camp police, committees for religion, music, education, sanitation, plumbing, food service, canteen, medicine and recreation. Everyone was obliged to serve on one or several committees from time to time.

Frank Willis, who shared a cubicle with Gerhard, had rented space in the same office building as the Alliance Press. The Christian Book Room was on the first floor and the Alliance Press offices and stockroom were on the third floor. Frank and Gerhard had often met for lunch or tea at the "You, Me Tea Room" in the same building.

"Shall we attend the lectures today or shall we join the baseball game?" Frank asked one day. It turned out that they took in both. And sometimes they took classes to learn Shanghai dialect Chinese or German. The education committee was doing its job!

The Japanese camp newspaper offered the only news the men received: Sweden had entered the war; New York City had been leveled to the ground; there were no cars or buses running in the States because of a gas shortage!

One day a missionary walked past Gerhard's bed and handed him a short piece of wire. He gave Frank a plug.

"Here," he said, "hide these in your stuff. They are radio parts that we are going to assemble today. That will enable us to get news from the 'Voice of America.' If 'our friends' come into the room while we're listening, we'll shout 'tally-ho.' Take your wire and plug and hide them." The scheme worked. But the comic side to it all was that "tally-ho" was called so often that the Japanese began to announce themselves with a loud "tally-ho!"

As a result of the radio transmissions, morale picked up in the camp because they were now informed of the real news—the allied victories. But it dropped to a low when the weather became warm and dysentery struck the camp. Medicine ran out as 500 of the 1,500 men, including Gerhard, succumbed at one time.

"Did you know that many of our good friends have died already?" Frank asked Gerhard one day as he listed off the names of missionary colleagues and others.

"That sure doesn't help a fellow!" Gerhard groaned. "Will you go out to the garbage can and look for my tin with a top? I think Robert Ding put more money in there for us today." Many Chinese farmers, such as Robert Ding, made a practice of coming to certain spots along the barbed wire fence when the guards were in other places. In this way, some of the internees were able to supplement the camp diet of watery rice gruel and a few vegetables with eggs, bananas, tangerines, bread or sometimes scrawny chickens.

"You sure have a real friend in Robert Ding," smiled Frank. "Without his money we would have starved long ago. I think I'll ask him to see if there is any medicine for dysentery in the city."

"Tell him to get it at the drug store near the

church at Wangkasha," Gerhard responded weakly. *If only I can survive the night,* he thought. Frank called Dr. Wallin and others to gather around Gerhard for prayer during the night hours.

As the last one prayed, Dr. Wallin leaned over to Frank and whispered, "I'll wait and see if he has any last words for his wife." Gerhard heard the comment and realized his life was slowly ebbing away. The thought came to him: *How can I give up with a lovely wife and four young daughters waiting for me at home? How can I fail our Chinese brethren and the Alliance friends back home who have been so kind to me? No, I must get well!*

Little did Gerhard realize that his name and face were well known in many Alliance churches, and especially in Dayton, Ohio, where the members prayed daily for him and the other internees.

The next morning Gerhard was awakened by a rooster crowing. Through the bullet holes in the roof, he could see the first faint rays of dawn. Psalm 71:14 came to his mind: "But as for me, I will always have hope. . . ." And Psalm 91:15-16: "He will call upon me, and I will answer him. . . . With long life will I satisfy him. . . ."

"Hey, Jake," a voice disturbed his reverie. Dr. Wallin was peering into his face. "You still here?"

"Why not! I told you the verse the Lord gave

me—'With long life will I satisfy him.' Yes, I'm still here."

"Then take this medicine that I got for you from under the fence. Pastor Chen brought it himself."

"Oh, God bless him!" Gerhard responded weakly. From that day on he began to recover. By now, heavier men had lost from forty to ninety pounds. Gerhard, somewhat light, lost many pounds too as a result of the cholera. Drug addicts and alcoholics, unable to buy drinks or drugs, soon died, followed by those whose bodies had been mistreated in other ways. Rolled up in cloth, they were placed in the earth in back of the warehouse with simple wooden crosses marking the spots.

It was a hot, sticky morning when the postman rang the bell in the foyer of the new apartment building where Alma, Grandma and the girls had moved in north Chicago.

"Oh, Mother, here is a cable from the internment camp in Shanghai. It says that Gerhard has a broken arm," Alma cried.

"Is that all it says?" Sarah Amstutz called back.

"Oh, my, I thought he had been tortured by the Japanese, but it says he broke it playing baseball!" Relieved, she laughed nervously. "Well, at least now we know he's alive and that's wonderful."

Some months later the postman once again

rang the bell in the foyer of the apartment building. Only Grandma was home this time. In his hand was another special airmail letter from Shanghai. Gerhard's name, it said, was on the next list of *Gripsholm* passengers to be repatriated!

Alma shot a letter back.

> My Darling Gerhard,
> We just had news this morning that you would be on the *Gripsholm* returning to the States. I cannot tell you how thrilled and happy I was to hear that! I did not know whether to laugh or cry. I guess I did both. With all my heart I praise our blessed Lord who has so abundantly answered our prayers. Yes, He is still on the throne. My heart is full of thanksgiving and gratitude to God for all His marvelous goodness and mercy and love.
> I have missed you so much. . . . I love you more than ever and you are constantly in my thoughts and heart. We are praying you will have a safe voyage home to us. Now for the news.
> Bette is married to William Linton III. He is studying in language school in preparation for being shipped somewhere in the Far East. Bette is going to have a baby.
> Doris is preparing to teach at the Toccoa Falls Elementary school in Georgia. She hopes to go to China as a missionary when the war is over. Winifred will go to Kentucky to work with the mountain people for her internship as she expects to return to China after nurse's training.
> Evelyn's boyfriend often visits her on weekends. She is working at the Edison Company. My brother Waldo helped the girls find jobs

downtown.

Remember, 'He maketh a way in the sea, and in the mighty waters' so we are entrusting you into His hands. Much love and kisses to the dearest one on earth to me.

'Til we meet again soon, Alma.

News that there would be an exchange of prisoners between the Japanese and the Americans set the camp ablaze with anticipation.

Gerhard and Dr. Wallin were playing checkers when the announcement came: "The names of those to be exchanged from this camp are posted." Frank Willis was closest to the posting site and discovered his and Gerhard's names on the list.

"Jake, Jake," he called excitedly, "we're on the list!"

"When will the exchange take place?" Dr. Wallin asked.

"Sometime in the middle of September."

After that it was like Christmas for those who remained in the camp. Everyone was giving away carefully hoarded food, winter clothes, books and other prized possessions.

The *Teia Maru,* which would carry the freed prisoners for the first part of their journey, was a fairly new French vessel which the Japanese had captured in French Indochina. Cabins were allotted to the sick, aged and women with children. Single ladies were crowded onto the floors in the salons and social halls.

THE DRAGON'S DEFEAT: TOGETHER AT LAST

Gerhard and the other men had racks in the hold of the ship. He would never forget the number: Hold A, Rack 208.

A December 1943 prayer letter detailed the trip home:

> We arrived in Marmagoa, a Portugese possession in east India by the middle of October, having passed Hong Kong, San Fernando in the Philippines, Saigon and Singapore. At each port we picked up internees. In Goa we received our first mail. Many laughed, others cried to learn of the passing of loved ones.
>
> We shall never forget the day of feasting after we were put on board the *Gripsholm*. We had a turkey dinner with all the trimmings. By 5 p.m. we were assigned to beautiful little cabins with nice beds and clean linens.
>
> After passing Port Elizabeth, South Africa, we sailed to Rio de Janeiro and were happy to receive more mail. All my daughters wrote letters of welcome, but only Alma was able to meet me in New York City. As the ship passed the Statue of Liberty we spontaneously burst into singing "America the Beautiful." Many wept unashamedly.

Many people from the Alliance headquarters gathered at the dock in New York, but Gerhard had eyes only for his beautiful wife.

"There she is, Frank, the little lady in the blue suit," he shouted, waving frantically.

What a welcome the Mission provided for the internees! After a sumptuous meal at a posh hotel, Alma and Gerhard enjoyed the pleasure of just being together again and chatting about loved ones on both sides of the ocean. After three years of separation, there were a lot of things to catch up on.

Then Gerhard took out his well-worn Bible. Slowly, deliberately, he read, "The kingdom of heaven is like unto a merchant man, seeking goodly pearls: who, when he had found one pearl of great price, went and sold all that he had, and bought it" (Matthew 13:45-46 KJV).

Gerhard closed the Bible and, taking Alma's hand in his own, bowed his head.

"Lord," he prayed, "we have done our best, traveling over land and sea to reach those of the Pearl, Your Church in China. May the Holy Spirit keep them through the dangerous years of war, persecution and suffering. We commit them into Your loving hands. Amen."

Epilogue

After World War II, the doctors did not feel Gerhard should return to China. So following a brief time with the Detroit Hebrew Mission, Gerhard and Alma returned to Pandora, Ohio to make a home for Sarah Amstutz and their two missionary daughters, Doris and Winifred.

Over the next ten years, Gerhard was an evangelist for the West Central District of the Alliance while Alma finished her required years with the Foreign Department in deputational ministries.

Winnie sailed for China in the fall of 1947 and Doris went to the Philippines in 1948. That same year, Evelyn married Kenneth Turcotte and Bette Linton had her third child.

The next year, Alma and Gerhard went to Chicago to be with Evelyn for the birth of her first child. It was a difficult birth and Evey's life hung in the balance. In the waiting room Gerhard experienced his first "tic" attack. The next day the doctors diagnosed his malady as "tic douloureaux," a deterioration of the tri-facial nerve, one of the most painful conditions an individual can endure. From that time on, Gerhard suffered frequent attacks.

When China fell to the communists in 1949, Winnie was reassigned to the Philippines and the sisters were together once again. The sisters returned for their first furlough in 1954.

During the furlough it was suggested that the senior Jacobsons spend the winters in Florida for the sake of Gerhard's health. God marvelously supplied a small bungalow for them and they opened a ministry among children in the neighborhood.

A highlight in the lives of Gerhard and Alma was the celebration of their 50th wedding anniversary in 1965. Many friends and loved ones, including Doris and Winifred, gathered for the special occasion.

Only a year later, the Lord called Alma to be with Him. She suffered a massive stroke and within one week, on May 26, 1966, passed away without regaining consciousness.

The shock for Gerhard was devastating. She had been the "rock" in the family, the one who cared for them all, the one who heard God speak directly to her—a great woman of faith and prayer. How could it be that she would go first? How would Gerhard carry on without his "anchor"?

The Lord miraculously comforted and sustained him with two wonderful dreams in which he saw Alma in heaven. After that, his life took on great spiritual strength and vitality.

Doris had been in the Philippines only two

EPILOGUE

years of her next term when the doctor informed her that her father had cancer. She returned to St. Petersburg and took a leave of absence from the Mission to look after him.

One day he said to Doris, "We suffered much with the loss of our things, five times—under communists, bandits and the Japanese. Both Alma and I were at death's door several times. Our little son is buried in Wuhu. But we found many who became a part of the Pearl, the Church in China."

On August 10, 1972, Gerhard confided to his friend Reuben Larson: "I'll be gone in a week." In the hospital he thanked the girls, especially Doris, for all they had done for him. Then he whispered, "Good night," and slipped into a coma. Seven days later he died. He was buried beside Alma in Pandora.

Among the verses he wrote is one called "God Has Promised." This stanza talks about heaven:

> There we'll see our blessed Savior
> And the dear ones gone before.
> Oh, what joy, I hear them singing
> And I see Jesus at the door.
> —Gerhard Jacobson

A List of Christian Workers from the Amstutz/Jacobson Descendants

Amstutz Line

Sarah Lugibihl Amstutz	Chicago Hebrew Mission, China	Six years

First Generation:

Alma Amstutz Jacobson	China	Twenty-five years
Edna Amstutz	Congo, Zaire	Career missionary
Rhoda Amstutz Thiessen	Pastor's wife	

Second Generation:

Doris Jacobson	Philippines	Career missionary
Winifred Jacobson	China, Philippines	Career missionary
Lois Thiessen	Costa Rica, Colombia, Guatemala	Career missionary
Vera Thiessen	Zaire	Career missionary

Third Generation:

Peter Thiessen	Philippines	Career missionary
Marilyn Amstutz Helms	Zaire	Two terms

(continued next page)

Jacobson Line

First Generation:

Gerhard Jacobson	China/USA	Forty years
Clarence Jacobson	Pastor	

Second Generation:

Doris Jacobson (see above)	Philippines	Career missionary
Winifred Jacobson (see above)	China, Philippines	Career missionary
Beatrice Jacobson Gardella	Pastor's wife	
Grace Jacobson Saltzman	Pastor's wife	
Robert Wilkinson	Bolivia/Pastor	
Joyce Wilkinson Prettol	Bolivia/Philippines	

Third Generation:

Curtis Wilkinson	Ecuador
June Wilkinson Ashley	Camp worker

China Update

The Christian and Missionary Alliance entered China in 1888 and for over sixty years maintained a high level of commitment to the Chinese people, including an overall total of nearly 550 missionaries. In the years prior to communist domination, the Alliance worked in Shanghai and seven interior provinces.

"Active forces during those years averaged eight-five missionaries and 225 Chinese church workers. By 1949, the Church numbered 8,000 baptized believers and many more adherents." (From *To All Peoples*, Robert L. Niklaus, Christian Publications, Inc., Camp Hill, PA, 1990.)

As of 1996, the Alliance is increasing its efforts throughout China, focusing on former Christian and Missionary Alliance areas of work and ten major cities across the land. This thrust includes radio programs, lay teachers and business personnel serving as professionals, and CAMA services education and social service projects. (From the *1996 Prayer Directory of The Christian and Missionary Alliance*.)